PRACTICE or TALENT?

What makes us musical?

LISA FAYE BROADHEAD

5678 PUBLISHING

First published 2014
5678 Publishing
PO Box 5678
Winchester
SO23 3BD

books@5678music.co.uk
www.5678music.co.uk
© 2014 Lisa Faye Broadhead / 5678 Publishing

ISBN 978-0-9931469-0-9

ALL RIGHTS RESERVED. This book contains material protected under International and Federal Copyright Laws and Treaties. Any unauthorised reprint or use of this material is prohibited. No part of this book may be reproduced or transmitted in any form or by any means, electronic or mechanical, including photocopying, recording, or by any information storage and retrieval system without express written permission from the author/publisher.

Designed by Paul Barrett Book Production, Cambridge www.pbbp.co.uk
Edited and proofread by Cambridge Editorial Ltd www.camedit.com
Illustrator Jan Sherwood www.thecreativitybox.co.uk
Production services by Wayment Print & Publishing Solutions Ltd
www.waymentprintandpublishing.co.uk
Printed and bound in the UK by 4Edge Ltd, Hockley, Essex

Contents

Introduction 5
Dedication 6

1. Music 7
2. Talent 10
3. Genes 13
4. Environment 16
5. The Brain 19
6. Practice 23
7. IQ – Intelligence Quotient 26
8. Experience 29
9. Child Prodigy 32
10. Earnest Practice and his Practice Tool Bag 37
11. Goals 41
12. The 10,000 Hour Rule 45
13. Chunking 49
14. Musical Ear 51
15. Feedback 55
16. Praise 59
17. Choking 62
18. Potential 67
19. Expert Musician 70
20. Passion 72
21. Butterflies and Voices 76
22. Practice Tips 78
23. Conclusion 86

The 5678 Music Tree 88
Bibliography 89
Index 92
Acknowledgements 94

Preface

I have written this book to help people reach their full musical potential by understanding the difference between practice and talent. Some people believe that they have no talent for music, but what is talent? What makes us musical – is it practice or talent? By analysing other factors, such as environment, belief, genes and how the brain works, we can begin to answer these questions.

I was inspired to research and write this book to help my piano and singing students understand these differences better. Practice is important but more importantly it is the *way* you practise that produces better results.

So, if you want to improve your musical ability but think you can't because you aren't talented enough, read on. And if you are looking for ways to improve your practice and get better results from your time, read on too...

Introduction

In my work as a music teacher and a singer, two words constantly seem to come up: **practice** and **talent**.

I say to my music students that they need to practise between lessons, so they can reinforce what we worked on in the lesson and move on to the next step during the following lesson. However, some students will make excuses for not practising, some parents don't know how to get their children to practise and some students and parents believe they don't need to practise at all because they are 'talented'. What is talent? Certain TV shows today present singing and music as a 'talent'; if you have that elusive 'X factor', it would appear that you don't need to practise at all, as you have that special natural something!

Would you call someone a talented dentist or secretary? They may be exceptionally good at their job, and have learned their trade, but we don't have them appearing on *Britain's Got Talent*, do we? Why is it then that music is seen by some as a talent or a gift, not an acquired skill that you work on or practise?

It saddens me when a student says that they aren't talented or that they can't do it. I remember a time at The Academy of Live and Recorded Arts, where I was studying Musical Theatre, telling one of the dance teachers '*I can't do it*', to which she replied, '*There is no such word as can't; you may find it difficult, but you will try*'. Those words have stuck with me for years and I hear myself now repeating them to my students today. How right she was; I now believe we can all do whatever we put our mind to. We are all born with the same instrument for singing, and learning to play an instrument is just like acquiring any new skill, for example riding a bike, walking, reading or writing.

So why don't we all sing and play musical instruments? For some, I suppose, it doesn't interest them. Why would that be? What makes us interested in something? Our genes? Then some believe they can't. What makes them believe that? Others just make an excuse as to why they can't do it and never even try. Why would this be? And if we are in fact 'talented' then what makes us that way?

Well, hopefully together we can discover some answers and explanations to these questions as we go through this book and help those budding stars of tomorrow or just frustrated musicians reach their full musical potential, by understanding the difference between Practice and Talent.

Dedication

This book is dedicated to all my students, past and present, some of whom practise and some of whom don't – but they will now! It is also dedicated to my parents for their unflagging support for me and my chosen career in the strange world of the music business. They have followed me around the world to see me sing, always encouraging me to follow my dreams. Thank you, Mum and Dad.

Thank you to Matthew Todd for his support and saying 'Just get on and do it!', and to a host of people who read through the first draft and gave me their continued encouragement, including Alistair Black, Yona Dunsford, Eryl Holt and Jan Sherwood. Thank you also to many people for their expert knowledge and advice along the way, including Mark Meylan and Emily Farthing. Finally, thank you to Debbie Wayment and her team for turning my first draft into this book.

1

Music

I have a lot to thank my parents for. In particular, the way they raised me and encouraged me to follow my interests, even if it meant not staying at my comprehensive school for 6th form, but moving away to London at 16 to study at The BRIT School – The British Record Industry Trust for the Performing Arts and Technology. This was the first school of its kind in the UK you could attend free of charge to study the arts, producing artists such as Adele, Katie Melua, Amy Winehouse and Jessie J. I was so nervous when I opened the letter saying that I had got in. I was sitting on my Mum and Dad's bed and can remember now how excited I was – the news meant I could go off and study dancing, singing and acting. I didn't want to be star or a celebrity but it was what I loved to do and I wanted it to be my career.

My parents were always supportive of me following my dreams and interests, and still are. They ferried me to dancing, drama and piano lessons. Mum encouraged me to practise my piano every day. In fact, there was no other option. Straight after school I would head to the piano and start whatever practice my teacher had set me for that week – scales, pieces, perfecting a few bars or even completing my music theory homework. I was fortunate that the piano was in a separate room, away from a TV and other distractions, so the focus had to be on playing. There wasn't much else to do in that room and Mum and Dad could hear whether I was practising or not from the kitchen, so the quicker I got on with it the quicker I could go and do something else. It became a habit. I grew up with my older sister, Julie, practising her violin and piano, so getting on with your practice was just something that you did.

8 PRACTICE OR TALENT?

I practised at the same time every day so eventually just did it automatically. If friends came round to see if I was 'going out to play' in those earlier years, Mum would tell them I would see them after I had finished my piano practice. Of course I moaned and grumbled but those protestations fell on deaf ears and so it became a habit to practise my piano as soon as I got in from school, or work it around dancing classes, drama groups, brownies/guides, etc. Every night of the week I was out doing some class or club, with Mum as my taxi... sound familiar? So how did my Mum get me to practise? Did she stand over me with a big stick or bribe me? Actually, neither. My Mum would reason with me, in a persuasive manner if she needed to, but because my older sister practised it was just what you did. My parents never allowed me to give up, especially when time was short around my GCSEs. I wanted to stop because of all the extra school work and revising. Mum wouldn't let me give in and now I am so glad she didn't let me stop, otherwise I really wouldn't be writing this book!

Enough about me and my experiences of my own practice; let's go back to our questions from the Introduction. Why wouldn't singing or learning an instrument interest someone? Music is everywhere in our lives, today more than ever before. We have iPods and phones that can play music wherever we are, and if we don't like the music that we are listening to, we can download a new album in seconds.

Music is played in shops, planes, on the radio and in films. We use it at weddings and celebrations, and for reflection at funerals. On our way to school and work we listen in our cars and today you can walk down the street and see people with headphones on listening to their music. In fact it is now even being played in some hospitals as it helps patients with their recovery. Music is the soundtrack to our lives. We use music for marketing, selling, escapism, entertainment, healing and communicating. It is everywhere, throughout the world, a universal language that we can all understand. Listening to a piece of music from another country we can tell whether the music is happy or sad; it conveys emotion that it communicates to us. So, what is music?

> **music** *noun* /mjuːzik/ a pattern of sounds made by musical instruments, voices or computers, or a combination of these, intended to produce beauty of form, harmony and expression of emotion

The word **music** originates from the Greek word *mousike* (*techne*) (the art) of the Muse. A Muse was one of the nine daughters of Zeus who presided over various arts. Today the word is used to describe an art form that expresses emotions by sequences of sounds in time, at various pitches, organised rhythmically, melodically and harmoniously.

However, music has been around since before the Greeks. Around 1.8 million years ago humans were making sound and singing as a form of communication (this can be deduced from fossil finds) and the earliest discovered musical instruments, made of carved bone, date back to between 42,000 and 43,000 years ago. It is believed that these instruments evolved from much earlier examples that haven't survived because they were made of wood and so rotted away. Music has been around for a very long time. It was a natural way to communicate and express emotion, so what has changed in today's society to make it the pursuit of a 'talented' few?

Talent

First of all let us look at the word **talent**.

> **talent** *noun* /tæl.ənt/ a natural skill or aptitude

The word talent derives from the Latin word *talentum*, an ancient unit of weight that equated to an amount of money and was used as a form of currency. A talent was about 80 pounds in weight and when it was used as money it was the value of that weight of silver. Talent = a value. So if we have talent, we have value.

The parable of talents is one of the parables of Jesus, where talents (money or wealth) are divided between three servants by a master for them to look after while he travels. When he returns, two of the servants have invested their talent and made more; however the third servant buried his talent, so all he could do was give back the original talent to his master.

So, what does this tell us? That whatever we are given – if there is indeed such a thing as a 'gift' we are born with – we need to work at it, develop it and invest in it, so that our talent can grow, increase and bring us wealth. We should not just keep it and believe that it doesn't need nurturing or it will never grow and your talent will have been wasted.

The word talent is used in a very different context today. We use it to suggest that someone has an inherent gift that they were born with; something that they don't need to work at, it just exists. We hear parents say, 'Oh my child is so talented', but still I ask, what is talent? In the television show *Britain's Got Talent*, contestants compete with each other over who has the best talent. Is training a dog to dance a talent? Or is it a skill, hard work and effort?

> '... call in the inspired bard, Demodocus. God has given the man the gift of song, to him beyond all others, the power to please, however the spirit stirs him on to sing.'
>
> **HOMER, *THE ODYSSEY***

In this excerpt the word gift has been used instead of talent, but the same inference is there. Here, we read that the character Odysseus believes that the ability to sing is a God-given gift; that Demodocus came into this world with the ability to sing and that in some way it makes him apparently superhuman, with a special power. Written between 700 and 750 BC, some 2,750 years ago, in many ways this opinion hasn't changed at all. Today in the 21st century we acclaim those contestants on *Britain's Got Talent* by praising their talents and in some cases even treating them as if they were gods themselves.

So is a talent or gift something that we are given before we enter this world? Perhaps this natural God-given gift explanation goes some way to explain why extraordinary performers are so rare, and why they are so celebrated. Surely God doesn't hand out these gifts to just anyone and everyone? So should they be celebrated?

Stop. I am not about to go into whether God exists or not – that's another book entirely. What this does raise, though, is the question as to whether we are sending out the right message. This suggestion that we are either born with a talent or not means what? Well, for those people who believe they don't have a talent, it can result in them not even trying. They will stop where they stand, saying 'We aren't the gifted ones' and so give up on the pursuit of excellence, not even try, and accept averageness. What a shame.

However, Liisa Henriksson-Macaulay, in the opening paragraph of her book *The Music Miracle*, gives us hope. She has discovered that scientific research now shows that all children have immense potential, contradicting the old myth that talent is only reserved for a select few.

12 PRACTICE OR TALENT?

Professor Graham F. Welch from The University of London agrees with Liisa, believing:

'We are all musical – we just need the opportunity.'

PROFESSOR GRAHAM F. WELCH

So where does this idea of talent come from?

3

Genes

Is anyone born to be musical? Or a singer? Or a musician?

As we can see, it has been believed for a long time that we are born with gifts and talents. Some people believe that our talents are given to us by God. However, others believe that our talents exist in our genes. These genes are passed on to us from our parents and determine who we are, not only physically, but also by generating things like our interests and our character. So might our genes be the reason why some of us are talented in music and some are not?

Well, let's take a look at what our genes are. Genes are in our DNA (deoxyribonucleic acid), which is found in all living things. DNA is like a chemical code that contains instructions, which we call genes. Genes instruct our body to produce proteins, which are our building blocks for things like muscle fibres, fingernails and eyeballs. Every cell in our body has our DNA, unique to us (unless you are an identical twin), and it can be found in a strand of our hair or in our blood. It is amazing to think that the same DNA can create hair and blood.

So if we are to believe that our genes give us our talents, then we should consider the old phrase 'nature versus nurture'.

> **Nature versus nurture –** This phrase was coined by an English Victorian, Sir Francis Galton (1822–1911), in discussing the influence of heredity and environment on humans (he favoured nature), although the debate itself has been around since the days of Plato and Aristotle in the 4th century BC. It suggests that it must be either nature or nurture that determines our abilities, character and behaviours.

14 PRACTICE OR TALENT?

In the red corner we have Nature, who is fighting for his parents. They gave him his genes and that is why he is who he is today! In the blue corner we have Nurture, who is fighting for everybody and everything. For it is her environment that has made her who she is today.

The debate has gone on for a very long time, with no clear winner until more recently. Gradually it seems that as science develops and we know more about our cells, genes and brains that the debate is coming to an end. In fact, a survey of scientists in 2014 said that the nature–nurture debate has outlived its usefulness and should be retired. This is because it is now seen that an interaction of genes and environment, nature and nurture, affect our development – not one or the other. We are who we are because of the influence of both nature and nurture, which is great news, so shake hands Nature and Nurture, you are both worthy winners. The result means no one has to stay as they are, as everyone has the ability to change if they want to. We have control over ourselves, and are not influenced by some ancient relative who couldn't play a note on the piano.

Genes are affected by our environment and also, we discover, by nutrition, the foods we eat or don't eat. Imagine three people baking a cake. You all have the same oven, oven temperature and ingredients (genes) – in this case, flour, eggs, butter and sugar. However, you each used a different flour – self-raising, plain and wholemeal. The result is three very different cakes. In fact, the chances of those three cakes coming out identical are very unlikely. What would make the three cakes identical? The same flour, (nutrition) for a start – and practice.

'The end product cannot simply be reduced to its ingredients.'
PROFESSOR PATRICK BATESON, CAMBRIDGE UNIVERSITY BIOLOGIST

Interestingly, Patrick Bateson's grandfather's cousin was William Bateson, who famously coined the word 'genetics' a century ago to describe the passing on of characteristics from parents to their children. Patrick is now updating that scientific viewpoint and readdressing our beliefs. His findings contradict the views of his late relative:

'Genes store information for coding the amino acid sequences of proteins, that is all. They do not code for parts of the nervous system and they certainly do not code for behaviour patterns.'

Research shows that genes on their own do not make us smart, musical or athletic. These talents are not passed down to us from our parents or grandparents. Instead, characteristics are developed as a result of, among other things, our environment and nutrition, and therefore are changeable.

So what is environment?

4

Environment

'Children will only develop as their environment demands they develop.'

DAVID SHENK, *THE GENIUS IN ALL OF US*

So if our talents aren't genetic, how are we affected by our environment?

Environment refers to where you live, how you live, whether you have any brothers or sisters, what interests your parents had when you were growing up – not because they passed them on to you in their genes (as we've already discovered this isn't possible), but because as a child you will be influenced by what is going on around you.

For example, my parents weren't interested in participating in physical sports, but my Dad is very interested in motorsport, especially Formula 1. So I grew up playing with cars, not dolls, and watching motor racing on a Sunday afternoon, going to Donnington Race Track to watch the car racing and knowing the names of drivers like Ayrton Senna and Nigel Mansell. I suppose this could have meant I might have become a racing driver. However, what must have influenced me more was being in Dad's Jag and listening to the French pianist Richard Clayderman playing on the tape player, or listening to Frank Sinatra and Nat King Cole on our car journeys. In the house I would sing along to the Carpenters and Shirley Bassey on Mum and Dad's eight-track (which they still have), and that certainly influenced me in the songs I sing in cabarets today, the songs I love to perform and the way I sing. In fact one day I danced and sang around the house so enthusiastically that I danced straight through a glass door!

This goes some way to answer one of our earlier questions. Why are some people interested in music more than others? The evidence is leaning towards the way that the child was brought up. Even before birth, music is influencing the child. A baby begins to hear from inside the womb in its third trimester, around 29–40 weeks. Primarily they respond to sounds their mothers make, such as speech and singing, but also to other external sounds and music too. Some mothers say that their newborn child will be drawn to music played during pregnancy, showing recognition by smiling or being calmed by it. Invariably mothers will say that their baby (within the womb) dances/moves when it hears a certain song, and research into early musical development suggests that all children enter the world with a range of musical experiences. This evidence suggests that we are not born as a clean slate. Equally, though, that is not to say that we are born musically talented.

'We aren't born with a "musical brain"; it develops through training, and this can be seen on MRI scans.'
DR KATIE OVERY, CO-DIRECTOR OF THE INSTITUTE FOR MUSIC IN HUMAN AND SOCIAL DEVELOPMENT, UNIVERSITY OF EDINBURGH

I have had the pleasure of hearing Dr Overy speak twice now on her research into how we learn music, its effect on us as humans and how professionals are facilitating music in education, health and other areas of our lives.

As we have already learned, we are aware of music before we are born. Most babies and children will automatically want to join in with music that is happening around them in their environment. We have all seen toddlers, barely able to walk, 'bop' on the dance floor at a relative's wedding or party when the music starts. They sort of bounce on their feet, bending their knees, feeling the beat and generally manage to do it in time (unlike most fathers who do 'dad' dancing). Does this in some way take us back to our ancient ancestors who naturally expressed their emotions and communicated through music? Children love music! They smile and giggle, feeling free to feel the music and do whatever they like; we applaud, encourage and think it's wonderful, cameras at the ready. Sadly, though, as many children grow up they are then told *'No'*, *'Don't do that'*, *'Sit down'* or even worse they are told that they aren't any good at dancing. How does this new environment affect the child? It stops them from doing that action.

Well, who can blame them? Who wants to do something they aren't good at or that they are going to be told off for doing? So, now our environment is having a negative impact on us. Our natural desire to move to the music is knocked out of us over a very short period of time and takes much longer to reinstate. This is the same with any early instinct. As the brain develops during our childhood, each neuron will produce many connections, but then gradually reduce down these connections to just a few strong ones according to how the brain is being used. If we are being told to stop making noise (music) or dancing then we break those connections. This could be another reason why we aren't all interested in playing a musical instrument or singing as we get older.

5

The Brain

The brain is a structure of organic matter that manages our movement and allows us to think and learn. The brain is forever growing, developing and changing. It is not a fixed entity. In fact, if we think about it we are not born with anything that is fixed: everything changes. Our hair, teeth, bodies, knowledge and skills all grow and develop. We learn to walk, speak, feed ourselves just like we learn every other skill, like football, writing, reading and playing a musical instrument.

It is estimated that at birth we are born with around 100 billion nerve cells or neurons – around the same number of stars that are in the Milky Way. A nerve cell or neuron sends and receives messages.

Basically, we learn like this. Our brain and spinal cord (our nervous system) are made up of neurons, which send messages (electrical impulses) around our body. Neurons are made up of a cell body, an axon and dendrites that

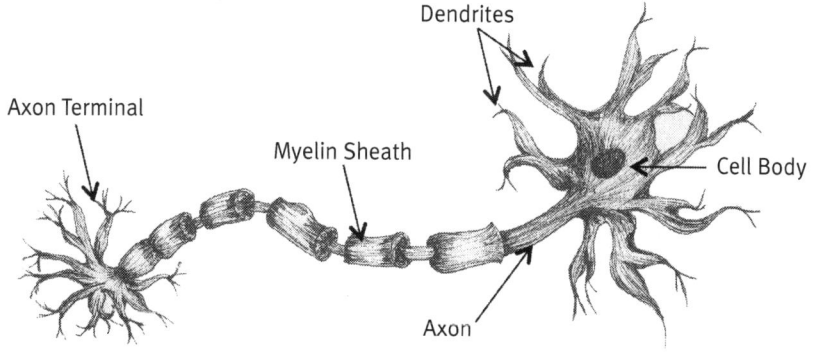

send and receive messages. The cell body is surrounded by dendrites that are a bit like the tentacles of a squid. These dendrites receive information, which is then passed along the axon, a long connection, ending up at the axon terminal, which then sends the message on further to another neuron via a synapse.

A synapse is a gap across which electrical impulses travel in order for one neuron to 'talk' to another neuron, i.e. send a message. This is a bit like the way we send text messages from one mobile phone to another across a network.

In most cases the axons are wrapped in myelin, a white fatty material. This wrapping is called a myelin sheath and it works like the plastic coating on an electrical wire, speeding up the conduction of the electrical impulses. The myelination means that connections are made more quickly, just like faster broadband connections or travelling on a motorway as opposed to country roads.

Max Myelin

I have two dogs, a black Labrador called Sam (three years old) and Max, an English Bull Terrier (11 years old). All my students love the dogs and saying hello to them is part of their lesson. Max, though, has always been a firm favourite. A big old softie who just wants a stroke, a cuddle and to sit in on the lessons, Sam sings along to the piano and singing lessons so loudly that I have to put him in the kitchen, where he sings along from behind the door! So meet Max Myelin.

Why? Well because he is white like myelin and, a bit like myelin, he makes connections quicker over time. Max makes those same connections every week when a student comes to the house, recognising faces each week, and making stronger bonds/connections with the students.

Myelinated nerve impulses literally jump from one gap in the myelin to another, much like Sam jumping up steps. It is much faster and takes less energy to jump from one gap to another rather than travel along the full nerve through unmyelinated nerve fibres.

Myelinated nerve fibres are called the white matter in the brain. Unmyelinated nerve fibres are referred to as the grey matter.

As we learn something or practise our musical instrument, the connections between the neurons for that particular activity get better at 'talking' to/connecting with each other, the more we repeat the activity. That is why we get better at doing a certain activity by repetition or practice. There can be several reasons for this:

A. The synapses become stronger and eventually permanent.
B. Additional synapses form.
C. More myelin is created, generating quicker electrical signals.

Some scientists believe that physiological changes take place in the brain during repetitive practice, hence its importance. Playing a piece of music over and over again means that the same messages will be going along the same nerves, creating layer upon layer of myelin, which in turn makes the connections quicker and stronger. This is why the more we practise the better we get. Beware, though, if you are playing anything incorrectly. Any mistakes will become myelinated as well, as the brain doesn't know right from wrong. The more you practise incorrectly the harder it will be to undo so it's far better to get it correct right from the start.

So does more myelin make us better pianists, singers and musicians? The answer is 'probably'. There are now studies that show musicians have larger and more myelinated nerve fibres that connect the right and left sides of the brain, and that those who studied an instrument from a young age have more white matter than those who didn't.

In 2005 Fredrik Ullén and others (Bengtsson et al., 2005) conducted an experiment where they scanned the brains of concert pianists, finding a direct link between the number of hours practised and the amount of white matter, myelin, in the brain. I wish I had known about myelination when I was younger: it might just have encouraged me to practise that bit more if I could have imagined my brain was getting faster and quicker as a result of my practice.

This research shows the importance and power of practice, that is to say repeating an action time and time again. Practice creates stronger and quicker connections or electrical impulses, which makes us better at that activity, as we generate more myelin.

> **'As children grow, their brains are customised around the uses they make or do not make of them.'**
>
> **JEFF W. LICHTMAN, HARVARD PROFESSOR OF MOLECULAR AND CELLULAR BIOLOGY**

So, the question is: What is affecting, influencing and creating these stronger connections?

Practice

Practice/Practise – The word derives from the Greek verb *prasso*, which means to perform repeatedly or habitually to achieve, bring about, execute or accomplish.

> **practice** *noun* /præk.tɪs/ the act of doing something regularly or repeatedly to improve your skill at doing it
>
> **practise** *verb* /præk.tɪs/ to do or play something regularly or repeatedly in order to become skilled at it

> Do not be confused by the two spellings! **Practice** is the noun form of the word – *I must finish my piano practice* – while **practise** is the verb – *I practised hard every night*.

We practise throughout our lives, although we don't necessarily call it that, or are aware that is what we are doing. The more we read, write, ride a bicycle, play a sport, the more we improve. All this repetition is practice: repeating a behaviour, system or an action over and over again with the aim of mastering, improving or acquiring a skill. If we want to master anything, we have to repeat it over and over again – in other words, practise.

As we have discovered from the previous chapter, this action of repetition builds connections in our brains that make us better at an activity. Does this then not imply that anyone can learn and improve, suggesting that our abilities are not down to talent? Comments like, '*I'm no good at maths*' or

24 PRACTICE OR TALENT?

'*I can't cook*' place talent at the heart of the problem, whereas it seems that practice is the key.

Just repeatedly doing an activity, though, sadly isn't the answer. What is really important is *how* the practice is done, not just the *amount* of time spent practising or the number of repetitions. If you have ever learned a musical instrument or singing, how much did you honestly practise? A quick five minutes after school or when your parents nagged you? Or perhaps you did the religious half-hour practice every day only to get nowhere or improve very little?

I asked these questions of some of my friends and here are their answers.

ALEX: 'I learned the violin. To start with about half an hour a day. This quickly dropped to about half an hour three times a week then about 40 minutes the day before my next lesson. However, if my sister, who played the piano, played with me then I would keep going.'

RICHARD: 'Between the ages of five and seven years old I practised very little (probably less than ten minutes on piano) between weekly lessons. When I started playing the guitar I practised far more (probably averaging around an hour a day). When I restarted piano lessons again at the age of 15 I still didn't practise very much (probably around half an hour a week) compared with the amount of time spent practising the guitar.'

'When most people practise they focus on the things they can do effortlessly.'
S. W. TYLER (PSYCHOLOGIST)

The key to effective practice is that it has to be focused and not just going through the motions, i.e. on autopilot. Autopilot means repeating the actions that have already become habit without any self-awareness of what we are actually doing, which results in very little improvement. We aren't focused on what we are doing, so therefore we can't correct any errors.

I remember practice like this, when I used to play through my pieces and scales as fast as I could just so I could say I had done my practice and go out to play with my friends. I would play through the pieces, not really making any progress except possibly memorising the pieces as I played them more and more. If I wasn't correcting my mistakes then all I was doing was reinforcing the errors, because now they were being memorised good or bad. Those connections were being reinforced by myelin.

Autopilot also kicks in when we believe that we know a piece of music. We play it through correctly, then a few days later it falls apart and we feel as though we've never played it before. We have gone back into autopilot and stopped being aware of what we are playing. We must exert conscious control to build additional expertise. If we simply cruise along on autopilot, believing we've got it, improvement stops and the wheels fall off, so to speak! This can also have an effect in an exam or performance situation. We may return to our old ways of playing as our brain slips into autopilot as we strive to cope with nerves and a new situation. (Chapter 21, *Butterflies and Voices*, deals with nerves.)

We can practise all we like but if we are practising the wrong things or just practising on autopilot we simply reinforce what is incorrect. **Practice makes permanent (whether that is right or wrong)**. We need to ensure that what we are practising, doing repeatedly, is correct and that we are practising regularly. The same time every day will help to establish a habit of practice, a bit like brushing our teeth, which we do every day without thinking. We also need to ensure that what we practise from day to day and week to week shows significant improvement.

What, I hear you shout, is significant improvement? That would be for you to decide. One practice it might be only getting a bar correct, but for other sessions it might be a whole line. Measured progress, though, is the key. Keeping a diary and notes of what was practised will help to make sure that progress is made day by day. Write down what improved, what was difficult and a plan for the next day or practice.

IQ – Intelligence Quotient

Some days you might come across a difficult section in the piece of music that you are working on and say to yourself, 'I'm not smart enough to do this'. You feel overwhelmed and want to give in as you don't feel capable. Much of the population link smartness to intelligence, knowledge and wisdom. In fact over the years the results of IQ tests have been used to determine how smart people are by purporting to show the intelligence we were given at birth.

So, how intelligent are you? If you type a search for 'IQ' into Google today there are various forms of IQ tests that you can take online in a matter of minutes. These tests are designed to assess speed of mental ability relative to others of a similar age. By asking questions on maths, shapes, words and other puzzles, your answers will determine your IQ (intelligence quotient) or how smart you are.

However, the Oxford Dictionary definition of intelligence is:

> **intelligence** *noun* /ɪnˈtel.ɪ.dʒəns/ The ability to acquire and apply knowledge and skills

What does an IQ test really tell us? It tells us that you have answered some tests either correctly or incorrectly and the result is your intelligence rated in a percentage form. This percentage is in comparison to the rest of the population similar to your age who have also taken these tests. The higher the percentage, the higher your IQ and if you score within the top 2% of the population, i.e. 98%, then you can join Mensa – for a fee!

Surely all an IQ test really shows us is how agile we are mentally at that particular moment in time, on that certain day, when we took the tests, compared with the rest of the population. What if you are having an off day?

Francis Galton, our English Victorian who coined the phrase *Nature versus Nurture*, first attempted to measure intelligence in 1883. He wanted to prove that intelligence was something set at birth, unchangeable, contained in our genes, by linking it to other heritable traits such as head size, height and good reflexes. He believed that smart, successful people were 'gifted' and had a superior biology passed on or inherited. His research was inconclusive.

Then in 1905 the French psychologists Alfred Binet, Victor Henri and Theodore Simon had more success creating tests to help and protect children not succeeding in school. The results would help by sending those children who received lower scores than those set for their age into special education, as opposed to putting them in asylums.

'Some assert that an individual's intelligence is a fixed quantity which cannot be increased. We must protest and react against this brutal pessimism.'

ALFRED BINET

In 1916 Lewis Terman, the American educational psychologist, invented the Stanford-Binet Intelligence Scales, one of the tests that we still use today. It was a development from Alfred Binet's test and became known as the IQ test, measuring a person's natural intelligence.

Sadly, none of these tests took into account any schooling or, indeed, home environmental effects on the person sitting the test. Instead they gave out the message that intelligence is something that you were given or born with, not something you've earned, and certainly not something that you can improve. It determined which schools children went to, whether they got into the army and even what careers they could pursue.

Today some of us are still using these tests as a benchmark for 'smartness' and it causes a segregation not only between cultures, but also between academic and creative people. Creative subjects such as music and art are not measured in IQ tests, so are we not negating 50% of the population?

Howard Gardner, a professor of cognition and education at Harvard University, believes that there is more than just one intelligence and developed the theory of multiple intelligences in the early 1980s through his 20 years of work. The MI Theory (Multiple Intelligence Theory) includes eight different intelligences, as shown in the table.

Spatial	Logical-mathematical
Bodily-kinesthetic	Interpersonal
Musical	Intrapersonal
Linguistic	Naturalistic

Gardner says that we have several different ways of processing information, not just the ones tested in current IQ tests, and that we might be strong in some areas but average in others.

New research shows we are not born with a fixed IQ (the ability to acquire and apply knowledge and skills). Intelligence can be improved and varied. In fact, very few of us reach our full intellectual potential in our lifetimes, so go out there and grow and learn. We aren't set in stone. The reality is that if you are finding a section of a piece of music difficult it is because it is new to you and you have yet to learn the information you need to play it.

Experience

We have discovered that our environment has an effect on both our genes and our IQ, so could our environment also be influencing our musical ability? Is there a possibility that how we respond to our surroundings and experiences determines to some extent what we excel at later in life or are interested in? Are we being nurtured by our environment? We know that the connections (synapses) in our brain become permanent when used regularly, so why wouldn't repeated exposure to the same experiences affect us too?

Sir Andrew Lloyd Webber, the composer, grew up in a house full of music. His father was a composer and organist, his mother a violinist and pianist, so it's no real surprise that he and his brother Julian grew up to be great musicians themselves, influenced by their environment and experiences. For me, as we've already discovered, dancing, singing and listening to music were part of my childhood, and now I work in the arena I love – music and entertainment. Looking back to my childhood, I also loved creating and performing my own shows, and I remember one Sunday lunch where I put together a show for my family at home. My parents obviously knew their daughter was destined for the stage and by default created a stage with their sunken 1970s lounge. The dining room became the stage, before you stepped down two steps to the stalls (lounge).

My programme on that Sunday lunchtime included playing the recorder, violin and piano, reciting poems, singing songs and dancing. Now, several years on, nothing much has changed, except the venue and size of the audience, although not even that on some days at the Edinburgh Festival Fringe, with my one-woman show, 'Dinner With A Diva'.

Generally what we enjoy doing as children is what we will enjoy as adults, whether that's art, music, mathematics, building or animals. This will lead us to the field and preferred career that we will excel at. It won't feel like a job, because we will enjoy it. Sir Kenneth Robinson calls this being in our element.

> '**Being in your element is about passion, you love what you do. When you enjoy what you are doing time flies, an hour can seem like 5 minutes. Being in your element is about tapping into your natural energy ....**'
>
> **SIR KENNETH ROBINSON (2001),** *OUT OF OUR MINDS*

Sir Kenneth Robinson is an English author, speaker and leader in the development of creativity, innovation and human resources in education and business.

What is the right medium/element/field for you ?

Think back to your early influences. What are you doing today that reflects earlier experiences? Think hard. For myself, I used to like writing and creating my own newspapers and at one stage wanted to become a journalist, so no wonder I am now writing this book. I also once wrote a book about flies as I carefully dissected them under my microscope! For this book you are now reading I have done a lot of research, which also takes me back to my childhood where I used to dig up/excavate our garden to find bits of pottery.

Ask yourself what you enjoyed doing or, even better, what you really enjoyed as a child – reading, discovering, building, creating or planning? Write out a list of at least five things to help you discover what might be your true element or field.

1. ....
2. ....
3. ....
4. ....
5. ....

Leonard Bernstein, the composer of *West Side Story*, discovered his element when he was a young child. He came downstairs to discover a piano in the hallway at home. His parents were looking after it for friends. With a child's curiosity he lifted the piano lid and played a few notes. As he pressed the keys and felt the sounds vibrate he liked it and spent as much time as possible creating such sounds. He had found his element and opened the door to his creative potential. He enjoyed making music.

Sometimes, though, we are wrongly guided towards an unsuitable field purely because we are good at something, but actually never stop to question if we enjoy it. Sometimes we don't enjoy what we are good at but simply carry on doing it because others want us to or because we feel we should. This route will never make you happy.

> For example, a very good concert pianist changed her career in her 40s because she suddenly realised that she didn't enjoy playing. A conductor questioned why she played and performed if she didn't enjoy it; she answered, 'because I'm good at it'. She was born into a musical family, showed potential in piano lessons, which led her to study for a music degree and go on to her concert career. She never asked herself if this was what she really enjoyed doing. The conductor advised her that night that 'being good at something isn't a good enough reason to spend your life doing it'. After her season finished, she stopped playing the piano, changing to a career as a book editor, which she loved and excelled at. She had found her element.
>
> Source of story: *Out Of Our Minds* by Sir Kenneth Robinson

We all have talents that we can develop, nurture or that we can shut off. Talents that are our field, our element, a result of our upbringing, environment and experiences – the things that make us tick. I do believe that finding and allowing our element to flow is the key to our future happiness. Imagine if everyone in the world found their element and worked within their chosen field. Wouldn't we all work more productively and be happier? Our experiences and environment do affect us significantly – how our brain develops and makes connections, especially in our earliest years. It appears that our exposure to experiences when young will have a bearing on our interests, hobbies and even careers as we grow up and go on into later life. So, what is your true field? What do you enjoy?

Child Prodigy

Where do child prodigies fit in? Don't they possess a gift that has been given to them by some superior force? They seem to have special abilities that come from nowhere.

> **child prodigy** *noun* /tʃaɪld prɑːdədʒi/ a child or young person who demonstrates a specific skill to a level beyond their years.

Child prodigies are people like chess champion Judit Polgar, golfing professional Tiger Woods and composer Wolfgang Amadeus Mozart. Leopold Mozart said about his son:

'A miracle which God let be born in Salzburg.'

There is no doubt that Wolfgang Amadeus Mozart was a child prodigy. Composing music and performing in concerts at the age of five, he wowed audiences with his talent. How he got this talent, though, is what I'm interested in. Was it a gift from God, as his father suggests? Let's look at the facts. Music surrounded Amadeus even before he was born. We know from earlier in this book that we hear and respond to outside music from inside the womb. Mozart's father Leopold was a violinist, composer and teacher. In fact, he was an exceptional teacher who self-published *Versuch einer gründlichen Violinschule* (*A Treatise on the Fundamental Principles of Violin Playing*) around the time of Mozart's birth. This book was highly acclaimed and its methods of teaching at the time were very unusual but have gone on to be adopted by teachers such as Shinichi Suzuki.

Mozart was listening to music before he was born, and he had a sister, Maria Anna, nicknamed Nannerl, who was four-and-a-half years older than him. Leopold taught her harpsichord from the age of seven, at which time Amadeus was only a toddler. Leopold focused his musical energies on Nannerl, who received expert tuition from her father and lots of monitored and encouraged practice from both parents. In a time where there was no TV, internet or electronic gaming, there was little distraction. When Amadeus was only two or three years old he sat at the harpsichord copying his sister's playing because younger siblings will naturally want to copy what they see their brothers and sisters do. His father saw his early interest and began to teach Amadeus at that young age, five years earlier than he had started teaching Nannerl. That is how, by the age of five years, Amadeus was performing along with his sister as child prodigies in concerts around Europe, fuelled by their father's ambitious focus on his children's success and the monetary benefits. Leopold was especially focused on Amadeus's musical progress because as a girl Nannerl would be expected to marry and discontinue her music studies.

Amadeus Mozart didn't have unusual genes, or a gift from God; he and other child prodigies have unusual upbringings. They have been exposed to their particular skill early on in life, had exceptional tuition, compressed thousands of hours of practice, grown up in an encouraging family and, most importantly, had a child's interest and will to learn. All these elements are needed to become world class, and a child prodigy.

'Talent is not the cause, but the result of something.'

DR K. ANDERS ERICSSON

Dr K. Anders Ericsson is a professor of psychology at Florida State University, and is an expert on expertise and practice. In his view talent isn't the start of something but the product and culmination of several things, including many hours of practice. Certainly my research points to the same conclusion so far. Don't get me wrong, I'm not saying that what child prodigies achieve is not amazing. Nor am I trying to belittle their achievements. It is an exciting prospect that children can become expert musicians at such a young age. I'm just the 'WHY'? girl. ! Just like when I was a child, I am still asking questions: where, when, what for, how long and why?

Creating a child prodigy
If we take what we have learned from Mozart's upbringing it should be possible to create a future musical child prodigy. We all want the best for our future generations so they can fulfil their potential. However, is spending hours in front of the TV or playing games on a computer creating child prodigies? They may become young computer games makers, producers of games, actors or script writers, as they are influenced by their experiences and environments, but are there other activities that they could or should be doing instead?

Some people believe that school will teach children everything they need to know; however, children are only in school for little more than six hours a day, depending on the school they attend. Let's do some calculations and comparisons.

School vs home
Based on children aged nine in a UK state school for 38 weeks a year (taking into account five teacher training days)

Children in school
6.5 hours per day × 5 days = 32.5 hours per week at school
38 weeks a year = 32.5 × 38 = 1,235 hours per year in school

Children at home
24 hours − 6.5 hours (at school) = 17.5 hours at home − sleep
(11 hours avg) = 6.5 hours at home
6.5 hours × 5 days = 32.5 hours (Mon–Fri)
2 days × 24 hours = 48 hours − sleep 22 hours (11 hours × 2 days)
= 26 hours at home (weekend)
= 32.5 + 26 = 58.5 hours at home per week

The result is 58.5 hours at home vs 32.5 hours at school per week. Of course you still have to travel to and from school, eat, wash and do homework, but that still leaves more time at home than at school in a week.

In a year, let's compare:

School = 1,235 hours
Home = 3,510 hours (awake) including school holidays
Sleep = 4,015 hours in bed (365 days × 11 hours sleep per day)

Almost three times as much time is spent at home as at school, which shows that children can do a lot of learning at home.

Even compared with UK independent schools, where some children spend around ten hours at school a day but have five weeks less at school, there is still twice as much time spent at home as at school.

School = 1,650 hours
Home = 3,095 hours (awake)
Sleep = 4,015 hours

These calculations show that we cannot leave the job of teaching children to schools and their teachers alone. Children need help, encouragement and support at home, in homework and practice. Look at Leopold and Amadeus; they worked for hours at home. Blame cannot lie with teachers and schools when a child doesn't learn, grow, develop or gain the grades that parents believe their child should be achieving. Schools and teachers are most certainly a starting point but teaching and learning is a many-handed job, with parents putting in as much time and effort with their children at home, as teachers, peers and schools put in elsewhere. This is especially important with music. Practice support at home is imperative to progress and success. We may only want Johnny to pass his Grade 1 piano, not become a child prodigy, but he still needs help at home. Usually a music teacher will only see the student once a week for half an hour, checking progress on work set the week before, building on the previous week's lesson and adding new skills. However, if no work has been done at home in between lessons then last week's work will have mostly been forgotten, because it hasn't been reinforced with practice and repetition that would have enabled the brain to make stronger and faster connections and build myelin.

School isn't for everyone; many parents are choosing home tutoring for their children and some are achieving great results. I do feel there is too much emphasis on 'if you don't do well at school your life is over', 'without your exam results … you won't get a job'. Well, it might be harder but we are only in school for possibly 14 years of our life, from 4–18 years of age. Not getting our exam results does not mean the end of our life, or that we can never get a job. Naturally the result improves our chances of gaining a college or university place or a job, but still there is no guarantee, especially today. An exam result merely shows what you know at that moment in time and, if you have a bad exam experience, it doesn't even show that. An exam result doesn't represent what you will know in the future, even tomorrow, and definitely not for the rest of your life. The result also shows what you didn't know at that point in time and where you can improve, grow and develop.

Based on figures for 2011, the average life expectancy in the UK is 80.75 years. This means we spend only 17% of our lives in school. In fact, based on our earlier numbers concerning the number of hours spent at school, it is actually only about 14%, yet some people allow this time spent at school to be the total of their whole life. We carry on learning way beyond walking out of the school gates and there is evidence that the more we keep learning the longer we will live.

What am I getting at with all this? The importance of practice at home, support and encouragement. We might not want our children to become child prodigies but I am pretty sure that we want them to achieve their best, their potential and enjoy the journey.

'Education is the kindling of a flame, not the filling of a vessel.'

SOCRATES

'When we say that someone is talented we think we mean that they have some innate predisposition to excel, but in the end, we only apply the term retrospectively after they have made significant achievement.'

DANIEL J. LEVITIN, NEUROSCIENTIST AND MUSICOLOGIST,
THIS IS YOUR BRAIN ON MUSIC

Earnest Practice and his Practice Tool Bag

'Expert practice is different. It entails considerable, specific and sustained effort to do something you can't do well or even at all. Research shows that it is only by working at what you can't do that you turn into the expert you want to become.'

DR K. ANDERS ERICSSON

Dr K. Anders Ericsson, the Swedish psychologist, conducted an investigation into the outstanding performance of violinists at the Music Academy of West Berlin in 1991. In short, the results showed that the more practice, the better the violinist. That doesn't seem surprising or extraordinary; however, it was a certain type of practice that he discovered was necessary for success, which he called deliberate practice. It was focused, of good quality and concentrated. The main importance was not allowing autopilot to kick in. If it did, errors would carry on undetected, and no progress would be made, as we have discovered previously in this book.

To help my students and remind us that we need to practise in a specific way and not allow ourselves to slip into autopilot in our practice I invented Earnest Practice. Earnest is a detective-like character who loves to solve musical problems and remind us that we need to practise in earnest. Just like a detective, we need to be looking out for problems, possible errors and searching out those clues that tell us how to make our music better. That means focus, attention to detail, finding the bad guys (the errors) and putting them in their place.

There are other practice tools, though, that we should have in our musical bag.

1. Mental practice

Now this doesn't mean mental, as in 'mad' practice, like playing or singing as fast as we can or running around the room like a crazy loon before we practise. No, it means that we are going to imagine, picture in our mind, ourselves playing or singing whatever we need to work on. Sports people and brain surgeons use this mental practice technique before they perform and perhaps as musicians we should be doing the same.

Jenson Button, the British Formula 1 driver, sits on an inflatable gym ball with a steering wheel in hands and, with his eyes closed, drives an imaginary lap of the circuit, going through the gear changes as he goes. He does this in real time, so when he opens his eyes he is pretty close to his actual lap time. As he goes he is picturing the bends, corners and straights of the track to help his actual performance on the day.

The brain doesn't know the difference between real and imaginary. Various experiments have shown significant improvement in actions carried out by those who only vividly pictured doing the activity. Effective mental practice, though, has to be as close to reality as possible. It has to be in real time and you must go though the actual movements you have to make. Just daydreaming won't cut it. You should see, hear, feel and even smell (if relevant) to recreate the actual situation or activity. As musicians this is a really useful tool, as we can imagine singing or playing a certain piece of music and feel where our fingers need to be, hearing the music in our head without physically doing it. We can also use this technique to help with practice away from our musical instrument. No more excuses saying, 'I couldn't practise because I couldn't take my instrument'. You have it with you all the time inside your head.

2. Fast food or 5★ practice?

Not that I am suggesting practice is edible, or that we should try and eat our music, but let's compare practice and performance to two different types of restaurants.

a) **Fast food restaurant:** The food is served very quickly, with not a lot of thought required. The service is generally pretty average and the food isn't all that great and is certainly not good for you. It is usually brown and bland – not much colour or taste. The restaurant is usually noisy, chaotic and loud and you can see the cooking frenzy happening.

b) **5★ restaurant:** The food will take longer to make as it is prepared especially for you and with care. The service is excellent and the food is exceptional, colourful, tasty and good for you. The restaurant is calm, luxurious, quiet and pleasant and you don't usually see work going on in the kitchen.

Now let's use these analogies in comparison with music practice.

a) **Fast food music:** Too fast, no dynamics or variety, performed without much care and not that great to listen to. The musician appears out of control and in a panic, perhaps.

b) **5★ music:** Performed with care and attention to detail, lots of dynamics and variety, fantastic to listen to. The musician is in control, relaxed and enjoying playing.

This comparison shows us that we must aim for 5★ every time in practice and performance. We should also aim to work like a 5★ restaurant – or perhaps a swan. With them we don't see the hard work that goes on behind the scenes or under the water to produce something. A swan swims smoothly on the surface of the water – it glides – but under the water its legs are paddling like mad. We must ensure that the hard work goes on before we have to perform, and under the surface or behind the scenes. We can't learn and perform at the same time, hence we practise before we perform.

3. Peak practice
a) **So what is the best time for practice?**
   As children, for my sister it was first thing in the morning before school and for me it was as soon as I got home from school. Now, however, it tends to be in an afternoon before I start teaching. Choose whatever works best for you, as long as it is at a set time each day, so it becomes a habit.

40 PRACTICE OR TALENT?

Schedule it into your day and aim for the same time each day. If it's scheduled, it will happen.

b) **Where to practise?**
Preferably a quiet and comfortable place away from distractions, so you can focus on your practice. Switch off the televison, computer or radio if they are in the same room and place telephones in another room, to avoid being disturbed. You should feel comfortable practising.

c) **How to practise?**
Like Earnest Practice. With a magnifying glass to search out any mistakes. Be a detective.

d) **How much practice?**
How long is a piece of string? Something every day is better than a last-ditch attempt before your next lesson. Practice should really take as long as is needed to master the next challenge that you and your teacher have set. If ten minutes have passed and you still haven't mastered it, stick at it a little longer; who knows, another minute or two and you might get it but if you walk away it will take even longer to get there tomorrow.

To recap, if practice makes muscle memory, or myelin, then it is better to:

1. Do your practice slow and correct rather than fast and wrong.
2. Use your magnifying glass, have error-focused practice – think, see, hear as you practise.
3. If errors occur, don't ignore them – fix them.

Remember:

'The easy route of practice leads to Mediocrity
The harder and challenging route leads to Excellence.'

DANIEL COYLE, *THE TALENT CODE*

11

Goals

In order for practice to be successful we need to have a goal to aim for. What do you really want to achieve and what are you willing to sacrifice to achieve it? For example, watching less television or limiting time spent on Facebook or computer games. *What Do You Want?* is a really important question, because if you don't know what your goal is, how do you know where to aim or when you have achieved it? It's a bit like going for a walk with no destination: how will you know which path to choose, where it might lead, and when you have reached where you are going?

What do you believe?
Do you believe you can reach your goal? If you believe you can then you will no doubt put in the hard work and practice required to achieve that goal, increasing your chances of success. However, if self-doubt is evident then there's a big chance that you won't get anywhere near your goal because you won't put in the necessary effort to get you to where you want or need to be.

Sacrifice
Generally, achievement at any level comes at a price: less free time, hard work, long hours, not seeing friends. This might not sound all that attractive, but this is the formula for success and it shows us that goals can be achieved by anyone and that they aren't reserved for the 'talented' few if we follow the formula. Our goal might be as grand as performing at the Albert Hall or recording a number one album. Or it might simply be to master a scale or play our favourite TV theme on our instrument. Whatever the goal, the same inputs are required: practice, time, effort and belief.

Belief

If you believe '*you can't*' or that you have '*bad luck*', then that is the message that you are sending to your brain and subconscious mind. In turn the relevant messages are sent around the body in reponse to this information. Our brain and subconscious mind only know what we tell them. For example, if you say '*I'm scared*', your brain will believe that and prepare your body for the danger it perceives must be about to strike, as otherwise why would you be scared? Your muscles tense, your heart beats faster, etc. However, if you believe that you can '*climb that mountain*', then your brain and subconscious will work to get your body ready for the goal ahead. Believing that you can achieve whatever goal it is you set for yourself is half way to getting there.

Equally, some people blame their circumstances or some other force that they have no control over for their bad luck, misfortune, inability and lack of success, whereas in reality they have created the outcome by not planning, believing, putting in the effort required, or listening to '*that other voice*'. Only you can put thoughts into your mind, so there is no way that you can blame anyone for what you are thinking. Not believing in yourself, your abilities or your potential is dangerous, as it gets translated into the physical form, like when I didn't believe I could sing a particular note.

As a teenager I believed that I couldn't sing above a top C. So I didn't sing above a top C for years, because that was exactly what I was telling myself. I would transpose music down, sing an octave lower, anything so I could sing everything in my 'big voice', what I later discovered to be my chest voice. Of course in reality I could sing above top C, it was just in a different voice, my head voice, which I didn't like to hear. It wasn't powerful and loud like Shirley Bassey. This almost lost me a role – Dorothy in *The Wiz*, a rock version of *The Wizard of Oz*, complete with gingham dress and pigtails – at the age of 18! I had a mental block about singing above a C. I think the fault lay in the fact that I could read music. Take the music away and I could have sung much higher, but I had told myself that I couldn't sing above a C – not in my big belty voice, anyway – so I never did. The musical director lowered the final song for me as, at 18, you just know everything, don't you? The real reason that I couldn't sing the note was because I had given up before I even tried. The required energy wasn't engaged, neither were my muscles receiving the message to get ready for the note. If a hurdler in the Olympics doesn't prepare to jump over the hurdle, they will run straight into it, which is what was happening to me with the high notes. I didn't prepare and therefore crashed straight into the note, reconfirming to myself that I couldn't sing above a top C. Focus and belief that I could do it were absent, and the fear that I wouldn't make the note created more unnecessary tension. This fear in turn caused my 'fight or flight' response to be activated, as my brain interpreted my fear as a signal that I was in imminent danger. This might be useful when we are being chased by a tiger, but not when we are merely trying to sing a note. It's hardly a life or death situation, but that is how our fear is perceived by the brain.

So instead we have to focus on the belief that we *can* achieve. We have to trust and throw caution to the wind. This is the only way we can learn, progress and develop. We have to challenge ourselves, because by staying safe and sticking to what we know we don't learn or grow, and in fact we will just stand still and actually get worse. If we aren't growing we are diminishing, and everyone else is passing us by as they learn and grow.

'We are what we believe we are.'

C.S. LEWIS, AUTHOR OF *THE CHRONICLES OF NARNIA*

Think back to a time when a peer or a teacher said that you weren't good at something, like maths, for example. If you are told repeatedly that you aren't good at something, over time you will believe what you are being told, reconfirming that the teacher was right. We have to believe that we are capable, and peers have to be careful what they say.

Believe everything that you play or sing will be great. Say to yourself, '*I am great*'; '*I can play/sing this piece really well*'; '*I have mastered it*'. You might feel silly saying these words out loud, but when you are alone who will know except you? Affirmations (which is what these words are) said out loud really do work as you are telling your mind that you are more than capable. Try it! What have you got to lose? Say either these phrases or your own several times, out loud, each day, and in a week see how different you feel.

Everything you have or are today was once a thought
There is evidence that the thing you think about most often is what you are or become. For example, can you think of a time when you thought you couldn't do something and that's exactly how it turned out? Close your eyes and see the story you told yourself. Now think about a time when

everything went well; did you believe in yourself at that point? Close your eyes again and put yourself in that positive place now, where it all went well. Picture yourself being successful and achieving. How does that feel? Good? Remember that feeling and next time you doubt yourself recall that memory. In fact we can recreate that feeling by creating an anchor – just like the one that keeps a ship attached to the sea bed, holding its position and not floating off. In a moment, close your eyes again and picture how great you felt when you were successful and achieving, then while picturing that moment press a finger and your thumb together quite strongly. That is now your anchor, and next time you need to feel successful you can press your finger and thumb together to take you back to that positive place and belief in yourself, your goal and your possibilities.

The 10,000 Hour Rule

How many hours do we need to practise to become an expert? According to Malcolm Gladwell in his book *The Outliers*, to master anything we need to practise for 10,000 hours. Now that seems an awful lot of time, and could mean some people never start as it seems such an unachievable goal, but let's put this into context.

The Beatles formed in 1957 when the boys were only 14, 15 and 16 years old and between then and 1963, when they had their first number one record, they had played many gigs including over 1,200 in Hamburg. A few calculations will show how they achieved 10,000 hours of practice:

5 years = 1,825 days
10,000 hours/1,825 days = 5 hours per day practice.

Now we can see how it became possible for four lads from Liverpool to achieve mastery as a rock band in five short years.

Even in my own experience, I realise just how important practice is. On one of my performances onboard a cruise ship performing my cabaret, *Streisand – The Main Event*, a passenger asked, '*How long have you practised for?*' I answered, '*Oh, a couple of years*', but when I actually thought about it I have been practising for many years. The show was originally created in 2009 and first performed in June of that year. Over the next four years I performed the show at the Edinburgh Festival Fringe, Trafalgar Studios in London's West End, on tour of the UK, and at Camden and Brighton Fringe Festivals before taking it to the ocean waves. I have been singing some of Barbra Streisand's songs since 1999 and many of the other songs within the show I had been singing for a lot longer than that, so I've been practising for at least 15 years. So that's 10,000 hours/15 years = 1.8 hours' practice a day.

Looking back at Mozart, his musical practice was concentrated into a very short space of time. Think of this as being a bit like orange squash. We buy it concentrated so we can get more of it into a smaller space and therefore it is stronger in taste. If we dilute it, it becomes weaker and takes up more space. So concentrated practice = stronger and takes less time. Also consider Dr K. Anders Ericsson, who stressed the importance of deliberate practice in order to progress and master a skill. It's fine to practise for 10,000 hours, but they don't count for very much if we aren't progressing. Those hours have to be focused, structured and measured. Remember Earnest Practice.

All our findings so far seem to be pointing to the fact that practice is outweighing talent in our quest to find out what makes us musical. Dr Shinichi Suzuki was a violin teacher who invented the International Suzuki method of music education. He believed that:

'talent is no accident of birth'.

SHINICHI SUZUKI, *NURTURED BY LOVE*

He developed his teaching alongside a strong belief based on the premise that talent, musical or otherwise, is something that can be developed in any child. He realised that:

'all children in the world show their splendid capacities by speaking and understanding their mother language, thus displaying the original power of the human mind'.

SHINICHI SUZUKI, *NURTURED BY LOVE*

Most us know how difficult it is to learn another language. At school we might try to learn French or Spanish – how many hours does it take? If we want to speak and understand another language fluently, then we are looking at around 10,000 hours. Suzuki's realisation was that if we can all learn our own language as a child, then why can't we learn any other skill? We aren't born speaking; we have to learn to talk just like we learn everything else. Here are some of the ideas that Suzuki uses in his music schools – you may notice some that we have already looked at:

A. The human being is a product of his or her environment.
B. The earlier the better – with not only music but all learning.
C. Repetition of exercises is important for learning.

'Man is the son of his environment.'

SHINICHI SUZUKI, *NURTURED BY LOVE*

I was watching a BBC4 documentary, *A Hundred Million Musicians: China's Classical Challenge*, where they looked at the growth and impact of western classical music in China, which was banned only 40 years ago and is now inspiring millions of children to learn a musical instrument. Over 50 million people in China are learning the piano alone. One parent said, *'My daughter practises 24 hours a day; apart from sleep, the rest is spent on piano practice and study'*. Lang Lang, a world-renowned young Chinese concert pianist who has played the piano at the 2014 Football World Cup, the opening of the Beijing Olympics and the Last Night of The Proms, says Chinese mentality is to work everything harder; you cannot slow it down. He was inspired to play the piano after watching the Tom and Jerry cartoon, *The Cat Concerto*, which shows Tom playing Liszt's *Hungarian Rhapsody No. 2* and being interrupted by Jerry. Lang Lang started lessons at the age of three years and now at 32 has a Steinway piano named after him. Lang Lang would put his success down to the Chinese practice ethic of working hard – the 10,000 hour rule, perhaps?

Obviously I am not suggesting that everyone has to practise for 10,000 hours to play well or to pass their Grade 1, for example. However, it does go some way to explain why some people take longer to reach a Grade 1 level than others. What we get out is all down to how many hours we put in. That takes me back to my earlier cake analogy. If we don't put in the correct ingredients we can't expect to get the right results. Equally if we don't cook the cake for long enough, then it won't be ready to eat.

Sometimes, though, shortcomings in a skill are put down as a result of the person's character or being natural so nothing is done about them. In fact, what we are discovering is that, through training and teaching, alterations can be made. Like training a dog, for example: we have to put in the hours of training to get the dog to do what we want it to do. Now though, through writing this book, I have realised that blaming any shortcomings on being

48 PRACTICE OR TALENT?

natural is just a lazy excuse – it means I don't have to do anything about correcting any problems, because who can change nature? I had better get back to that dog training and prioritise my time to see what an hour's practice every day can achieve. Max and Sam, watch out!

There is no getting away from the fact that if we want to be a better musician or better at anything, we have to practise by repeating the activity correctly many, many times. Otherwise, as Earnest Practice says, *'They don't mean anything'*.

13

Chunking

All this talk of 10,000 hours of practice, though, can seem overwhelming. Some people might feel that if it takes that much work then they simply won't bother at all, while others might blame a lack of talent. It is a little like when we look at a new piece of music for the first time. It is all unfamiliar and unknown – where do you start? The answer is that we aren't expected to practise for 10,000 hours in one session. We need to break it down into smaller time slots so it is more manageable and achievable. This is called **chunking** and can be applied to the piece of music by breaking it down into bars or lines to make it easier to manage. Just like a chocolate bar that is made up of chunks; you wouldn't try to eat the whole bar in one mouthful, would you? It is far more manageable in bite-sized chunks.

Generally speaking we like to chunk things into threes. For example, we usually memorise phone numbers in three parts: the area code is the first and then we divide the last six digits into two lots of three – 01863 352 837. Books usually have an introduction, content and then a conclusion, and even a piece of string has a start, a middle and an end. Music is usually made up in this way too. Look at or listen to a piece of music and see if you can divide it into three. If the three chunks feel too large, then you can subdivide each section into a further three chunks, and so on until the chunks are workable. This might mean note by note, word by word, bar by bar or line by line. This process will make working on a new piece of music or song more manageable and, once you have mastered the smaller chunks, you can start putting them back together to make larger chunks, until you get back to the whole piece. You will actually find that you learn faster when problem solving in this way by taking small and steady steps, rather than trying to tackle the whole thing.

Chunking practice

Not only can we chunk a piece of music, but we can also chunk our practice. If we see practice as one big chunk we can be overwhelmed by how much there is to do, so we need to break it down into smaller areas of what needs to be worked on. It might break down into: 1) pieces, 2) scales, 3) sight reading. Then it can be broken down into smaller chunks again. A) right hand, B) left hand, C) hands together or a) first four notes, b) next four notes, c) all eight notes.

Take your time and chunk. You can't rush a cake baking, as we've already stated, as it just won't turn out right. If you speed up the cooking time it will come out under-done and if you turn up the heat it will burn. It's exactly the same for music. If we try to speed up the process we won't be ready and if we turn up the heat our fingers will get burned. We can also bring in another useful principle here – the Pareto Principle, also known as the 80/20 rule.

80–20 rule

This magic formula was named after Vilfredo Pareto, an Italian economist, sociologist and philosopher, who in 1906 noticed that 80% of the land in Italy was owned by 20% of the population and that 80% of peas came from 20% of the pods in his garden. This principle has been developed to suggest that roughly 80% of all results come from 20% of the effort or cause.

We can apply this rule to music. We should be identifying which 20% of our effort will produce 80% of our productivity, otherwise we could be wasting 80% of our time. Thinking of our practice with this rule in mind we can use our time practising to better effect by working on high-priority aspects. Our nature is undoubtedly to practise the things that we already know, but is this helping us to improve? No. Think about this rule in relation to one of your pieces. You will probably find that you can play 80% of it, but there is 20% that needs more work and you probably spend the least amount of time on whatever needs the most work.

To help improve practice, here are a few suggestions:

1. Work out the 20% of a piece that you can't do and practise that.
2. Spend 80% of your time working on the part that you find difficult, not 20% of the time.
3. Work out the 20% of scales that you find difficult and practise them.

14

Musical Ear

In trying to answer our question as to what makes us musical, we find there is a group of people that just firmly believes that they aren't. Where do these beliefs originate?

Let's take a look at them. I know many adult singing students and even a couple of members of my choir who didn't sing for years because a teacher or parent told them they couldn't sing and that they should be quiet. Some were even told that they didn't have a musical ear and that they were 'tone deaf'. They were instructed to stand in the back row of the school choir or assembly and mime. What effect did these negative comments from teachers and public humiliation in front of friends generally create? A lifelong belief of musical inability, to such an extent that they won't sing in public, or even at all, for a very long time, if ever.

> **'A negative life event such as being labelled tone deaf can result in ongoing negative emotional responses in similar contextual situations.'**
>
> DAVIDSON, JACKSON AND KALIN, *EMOTION, PLASTICITY, CONTEXT AND REGULATION*

We will look at the power of feedback, its effects and how to give better feedback in the next chapter, but for now let us unravel the term tone deafness.

What is tone deafness?

> **tone deaf** *adj* /təʊnˈdef/ an inability to distinguish differences in pitch in musical sounds when hearing or producing them

Generally speaking it is a term that has been incorrectly used for years to label out-of-tune singing. In fact only a very small fraction of the world's population is tone deaf or suffers from the condition amusia, which is its medical name. Tone deafness or amusia is actually a musical disorder which means that the sufferer has an inability to produce and comprehend music. Sufferers report a lifelong failure to recognise familiar tunes or even differentiate one tune from another. They complain that music sounds like a 'din' – like the clatter of pots and pans – and will often avoid places where music is played.

There are two forms of amusia: congenital amusia, which is a result of an anomaly at birth, and acquired amusia, which is a result of brain damage later in life. Adults regularly use the excuse, '*I'm tone deaf*' when I am trying to encourage them to join in a singing workshop or team-building event. Surely I can't have most of the world's amusia sufferers in one of my workshops? Could it be that some people are using it as an excuse?

Why can't you sing in tune? It can be down to several reasons:

- Your parents sang out of tune to you as you were growing up. This resulted in you repeating what they sang to you, thinking it was correct.
- You haven't really listened to what is being sung or played to you. You need to really listen, pay attention and correct yourself. Be honest.
- You were not surrounded by music as you grew up.

When I was studying musical theatre at ALRA (Academy of Live and Recorded Arts), there was a girl who struggled to hold a tune – to sing in tune. On speaking with her I found out that she had grown up in a house without music. Her parents didn't play or listen to music, so she had no need to sing or put a tune together and hadn't developed a musical ear.

> **musical ear** *noun* /mjuːzɪklɪə[r]/ The ability intuitively to learn or appreciate music, esp. with the ability to distinguish off-key and off-pitch music

She was learning for the first time at drama school to put notes together, listen to music and aim to replicate with her voice the sounds that she heard. This repetition of sound, or practice, resulted in her learning a new skill – she was learning to sing.

Correcting out-of-tune singing

We can correct out-of-tune singing by replacing it with in-tune singing. Our brains are similar to a record – the thin black vinyl disc used for recording music that preceded CD and mp3 players. A record has the music ingrained into the vinyl just like our brain has what we have learned ingrained in its connections and then cemented in place by myelin. If we take that vinyl and scratch it with a pen or knife, so we cut through the rings, we are rewriting the music and that record will never be able to be played in the same way again. That is exactly what we need to do with how we sing. We need to scribble through the old habits that produced a sound, so we can lay down new ones. It is only repetition or practice of the old way that has got us to where we are today. Now we have to repeat a new action/technique/sound to move us forward.

It's a bit like getting Max Myelin to let go of a favourite old bone or toy. It's pretty difficult but in the end he will swap old for new!

As we get older it can be harder to create new habits, but harder doesn't mean impossible. I have taught adults to play the piano and learn to sing when they have been told they can't. It just takes a little longer as we become older, because we get out of the habit of learning new skills and practising.

So no more excuses that you are tone deaf... unless you bring me a doctor's note to prove it!

A musical ear should not be mistaken for musical ear syndrome.

Musical ear syndrome (MES)

This is a condition that affects one in 10,000 people over 65 in the UK (BBC1 North West Inside Out 17 December 2012) and is generally, but not always, associated with people who have lost their hearing or are hard of hearing. These people suffer from hearing musical hallucinations – music that isn't really there. That is, the music is not there externally; the sounds are generated in the brain. Usually the music is from their youth, and would be music that was heard or sung repeatedly, like Christmas carols, the national anthem or Happy Birthday.

Ear worms

These are not as serious as MES, as you can get rid of these out of your head. An ear worm is the name for those annoying snippets of a song or piece of music that get stuck inside your head, repeatedly playing over and over again, on a perpetual loop – like the last song that you heard on the radio.

15

Feedback

'Every wrong attempt discarded is another step forward.'

THOMAS EDISON

As we have learned from the previous chapter, the right sort of feedback is vital in nurturing our musical ability in its infancy. It is also really important in our development, because if you don't know what you are doing wrong or right you can't know what to improve upon. Feedback is vital for progress and to promote practice. However, with the current TV shows like *X Factor* and *Britain's Got Talent* we are made to view feedback as bad. The audience boos the judge who gives any negative feedback and generally the participant doesn't accept it graciously. This may be because it's a TV show, but it might also be because this is the first time the contestants have had any honest feedback. If parents and friends have only ever said that they are great, they may have a false view of themselves and their ability and therefore are unable to accept the true feedback.

We are given external feedback on almost a daily basis. Somebody will have an opinion on how we have carried out an activity – '*Well done*' or '*I would have done it this way*' or '*You could have done better*'. In work, school and at home, feedback is part of everyday life. In music, our feedback comes from our teachers, audience and examiners, and can feel positive or negative.

Positive feedback
So what might positive feedback look and sound like?

> Applause
> Tick or star   A prize
> Certificate
> A compliment – Well done, You did well, You were great
> Recommendation   Smile
> Laughter
> Pass/Merit/Distinction or A, B, C.

What can we do with this feedback?

- Make a note of what you did that got positive feedback.
- Keep a notebook or diary of the things that go well.
- Ask the person what they liked.
- Try and replicate the action that got positive feedback.
- Apply what went well to future activities.
- Build on it – can you be even better next time?

Negative feedback
What might negative feedback look and sound like?

> A cross
> A comment – You need to…, This could have been better…
> Silence
> A fail in an exam or test
> A frown or sigh
> Writing in red ink

What can we do with this feedback?

- Make a note of what you did that got negative feedback.
- Keep a notebook or diary of the things that don't go well.
- Ask the person what they didn't like.

- Don't do it again.
- Apply feedback to future activities.
- Build on it and make it better next time.

Using feedback

We often do nothing with the feedback that we are given. We think we do; we acknowledge what the person is saying, nod in agreement and say that we understand. Yet in reality it goes in one ear and out of the other, or our inner voice gets involved, again commenting on what is being said, for example *'they don't know what they're talking about'* or *'why don't they like it my way?'*, giving you its own feedback. The result is no action being taken, so no change is made, and we carry on in exactly the same way as we did before.

This can be true even with positive feedback. A compliment has been made about our work; however, we brush it off, or accept it grudgingly. Why do we do nothing with this feedback? What could we do with it?

Using feedback is very different from just accepting it. Don't make the mistake of reflecting on the feedback before acting on it, or you are more than likely not to act on it at all. Apply it first and then reflect on whether it worked or not. We improve how we act on feedback the more often we do it and the quicker and more frequently we implement it. So get into the habit of applying feedback when it's given and see what improvements are made.

Tips

Feedback doesn't only have to seem negative to improve a weakness. It should also be positive, stating what is correct and well done. Try to see feedback as being in three parts:

> A – identify what was correct
> B – replicate that, again and again
> C – try and apply that elsewhere.

We can only focus on a few things at a time, so limit the amount of feedback. Remember from earlier that we like to do things in threes, so limit feedback to three pieces at any one time. Ensure that feedback is consistent and not overwhelming, especially to yourself and change *'don't'* statements into *'what to do'* statements. For example, change, *'Don't play so fast'* to *'Take more time*' or '*Slow down*'. Providing a solution to a problem is better than just saying what the problem is, i.e. '*Don't play so fast*'. Our brain only hears the command of the action, i.e. PLAY FAST, it doesn't hear DON'T. When you see the sign, '*Don't Play On The Grass*', what does it make you want to do? Play on the grass, of course, because that is the action that your brain is seeing and registering, whereas until you read the sign, you didn't want to play on the grass at all. So instead of using the word '*don't*', say what you want to happen, for example play more slowly, take care, etc.

Be specific and make the solution achievable
It is really important to check that any feedback given to others has been understood. If you just ask them they can say '*Yes*' but maybe not understand at all. Get them to tell you in their own words what they have understood, repeating the feedback back to you. Also, by saying the feedback out loud they have more chance of carrying it out as they are affirming to themselves. Making an **affirmation** is a great thing and is very productive. Finally, get them to prioritise the feedback, so they decide what is the most important thing to focus on. They are more likely to carry out the feedback if they see it as their idea.

A word of caution
1. It is really important not to blame character; instead, state the fact. If you knock over a glass of water, you aren't clumsy, you knocked over a glass of water, that's it.
2. Don't judge, encourage. We need to be careful not to instil our own pressures and judgements on to others.
3. Feedback shouldn't come in the form of criticism. This can lead to a fear of feedback and fear of using our initiative and imagination, limiting individuality. People would rather blend in than stand out and be criticised, which can often cause irreparable damage and inferiority complexes.

We have to be honest but in a constructive way.

16

Praise

'Praising children's intelligence harms their motivation and it harms their performance, whereas praising their effort has greater effect.'

CAROL DWECK, *MINDSET*

Carol Dweck is a Stanford University social psychologist who has studied the impact of praise on student achievement. Her research shows that you should praise a child for their actions, not their traits. Praising traits, such as *'You're smart'*, *'You're musical'* makes children feel superior and great for the moment, but it's dangerous. If students then hit a problem they can feel dumb or a failure. We think we can offer permanent confidence by offering praise for brains or talent, but it actually has an opposite effect. When they are faced with a problem or challenge, they blame themselves if they can't solve it or work out how to play/sing a section of a piece of music. They don't believe that there is another solution and think they can't and therefore won't try. They will blame their ability. However, in contrast, praising effort and viewing challenges or difficulties as a good thing means that we believe we can improve, learn and develop and are in charge of our future potential. It's imperative to focus on skills and achievements gained through effort, otherwise we are robbing opportunities, challenges and future potential.

So, does praise develop motivation to be better and therefore promote practice? It certainly works for me from my own experience. I have always striven to work harder for praise, not following a stern telling-off or criticism. I prefer the carrot, not the stick. However, we are all different. Some strive to work better at the thought of an achievement, a goal or a prize, whereas others seem to respond to a telling-off, a raised voice or a threat of losing a treat. I work via praise and always have done. If a teacher (or anyone else, for that matter) said something I did wasn't good enough or right I just didn't like it. I generally also didn't do anything about it to make it better. Whereas through encouragement I did, and if I thought I was pleasing that someone, I would work hard to gain their praise. I suppose that's the beauty of a great teacher. They work out how the individual student works and plays to their needs to get the best out of them.

There is research that suggests that what we say to children and in fact to adults, can have a detrimental effect on them. Praise a child, tell them they have worked hard, done well, etc. and they will achieve. Tell a child they are thick, stupid, no good, naughty... well, I think you can see where I am going with this one. Words are very powerful. If we keep saying the same thing to someone, at some point they will start believing it. So make sure that the words we are saying are the right ones – encouraging words.

'Children Will Listen', a great song by Stephen Sondheim, from his musical *Into the Woods*, relates this wonderfully and the words of that song ring true for me. Children learn from their elders and peers by copying and imitating. What we do and say, whether good or bad, children not only listen to but watch and copy, hence children very often become mini versions of their parents. Look at yourself and see how many traits are similar to those of your parents – your stance, habits, voice? If a parent raises his or her voice, then don't be too surprised when the child does too. To them this is the right way to behave because that is what they have been taught. Children are a clean slate upon which we write; we must make sure we write carefully as it is not so easy to erase what has been written. Not like chalk, rather like indelible ink.

Praise can come in the form of letters – A, B, C – or words like Pass, Merit or Distinction, and there can be a problem here in that they don't tell us much about the person's abilities or the process by which they got there. I suppose a higher mark should reflect a better process, like earnest practice, and a lower grade means not enough practice or not the right sort. However, this might not always be the case.

What does fail mean? None of us wants to fail and we should always strive to succeed and pass, and do our very best. However, fail doesn't mean you are a failure – the end of your life or your musical aspirations, or any aspirations for that matter. It merely means that you haven't yet attained all the elements you need for that particular test and shows what you need to go ahead and learn, or go back and relearn. Failure is good, when we learn from it.

> **'Failure is simply an opportunity to begin again, this time more intelligently.'**
>
> **HENRY FORD**

We all need to learn that there is more than one way to solve a problem or interpret a result. If we fail we shouldn't give up. Would we have ever learned to walk if this was the case? No, we would have just stayed where we fell, as learning to walk meant falling down and failing with every new step to begin with. Learning to walk isn't a talent, it is a skill we have to learn by repetition and trial and error. Sometimes we have to try a whole range of different approaches to reach our desired goal. Persistence is key and as we keep trying and trying again, our practice and learning skills improve.

The NACCCE (National Advisory Committee on Creative and Cultural Education) report 1999 points out that:

> **'the first task in teaching for creativity in any field is to encourage young people to believe in their creative potential, to engage their sense of possibility and to give them the confidence to try'.**

Many famous and successful people failed at first. Walt Disney was fired by a newspaper editor because he lacked imagination and had no good ideas. Elvis Presley, the King of Rock and Roll, was fired after just one performance and told, *'You ain't going nowhere son. You ought to go back to drivin' a truck'*! Even Ludwig Van Beethoven struggled with his violin practice as a child. His teachers felt he was hopeless and would never succeed on the violin or composing.

> **'Allow children to fail. If failure is not allowed, children will tend to play it safe and never take creative risks.'**
>
> **CRAFT, JEFFREY AND LEIBLING, *CREATIVITY IN EDUCATION***

Choking

Think back to the bar of chocolate and its chunks. If we attempt to eat the whole bar we might choke, as it is overwhelming. That's exactly what happens to us when we try to take on too much or we try too hard. Instead of letting what we know or what we have practised happen, all previous knowledge seems to disappear and we choke.

Imagine choking; what happens? We are trying to swallow, breathe, carry out an action that we do naturally all the time but there is a blockage; an obstacle is in the way. This causes us to panic, because we can't breathe; we become more tense and all we can think about is what we can't do – breathe. I know this only too well, as while waiting for my sister at her piano lesson one day I was offered a sugared almond by the teacher's husband, which I took and began to suck. Then he offered me a Jaffa Cake, which I also accepted, even though I hadn't finished the sugared almond. You can guess what happened! I was eager to eat the chocolate-covered Jaffa Cake, so I swallowed the remaining sugared almond, only it got stuck. My sister's music lesson came to a swift halt as I was whisked off to A&E. My Mum still has that sugared almond in a jar (being from Yorkshire we throw nothing away) and strangely enough I'm not such a fan of sugared almonds or Jaffa Cakes now.

The lesson learned is obviously don't be greedy! When we try too hard, we cause a blockage in the natural flow of whatever activity we are doing, in our case music. Then, because the natural flow of what we thought we knew is obstructed we begin to panic, creating tension and loss of focus on the music. We can only focus on one thing at a time and that is on the choking that is happening.

> 'Our thoughts have a powerful effect on our body and therefore our voice. A tight mind will lead to a tight body and a tight voice.'
>
> BARBARA HOUSEMAN, VOICE AND ACTING COACH, *FINDING YOUR VOICE*

Effects on our performance

Trying too hard stiffens fingers, arms, shoulders and neck, which makes playing a musical instrument or singing more difficult as this tension then affects the rhythm, tone and dynamics and the music can't flow. Have you ever wondered why we don't perform as well in our lessons or exams as we do at home? Well, precisely for this reason. We are trying too hard to demonstrate what we have practised at home. How many times have I heard, *'it went fine at home'* and I remember saying those exact words to my piano teachers. We start choking and the fluidity that we usually play or sing with goes of out the window. Unfortunately those situations where we want everything to go perfectly, like in a lesson, exam or a performance, are exactly those times when we will try too hard.

To help counteract the choking effect we need to not try so hard. This is easier said than done. Instead, be aware of what you are doing without judgement and without actually trying to do something. Too much effort can cause tension, so by being aware we can keep track of any unnecessary effort. Be curious and interested in what you are doing, not judgemental and doubtful; it will be more fun and productive. Be generous with yourself – don't beat yourself up trying to do something. If that was someone else trying and you were looking on, wouldn't you be encouraging and supportive? So do the same for yourself. What we need is a plan to help combat choking when it rears its ugly head and put ourselves in the optimal position to perform our best, and be able to show what we have practised. We need to plan ahead, so here are some suggestions.

1. **Anchoring.** When you are practising at home, or wherever you practise, how does that feel? Take a few minutes to take note of how you feel – relaxed, warm, confident, happy? How is your breathing – calm, relaxed, normal? What sounds are going on around you? Is there traffic passing by outside? What smells are there? Is someone cooking in the house? Look around the room and make a mental note of some features in the room, like pictures on the wall, the colour of the walls, if the cat or dog

is in the room with you. It would be a good idea to write down your observations, or at least close your eyes so you can hold these pictures and feelings in your head, as we are going to use them later on. We could also make this another anchor, as we did earlier. Press your thumb and finger together to help lock yourself in this place of calm.

2. **Creating a picture.** When you are practising, spend some of your practice imagining that you are in the exam or performing. Really picture what it might be like. How many people are listening to and watching you? How do you feel? What does it sound like? What does it look like? Draw a really strong mental picture of yourself in that situation once or twice when you are practising – even walking into the room, or onto the stage. Go through it all in real time in your head. Athletes practise this way and then, when they enter a stadium to participate, they put themselves back in the comfortable space of their practice area, which helps stop the choking effect.

3. **Relax.** When you are in an exam or performance situation, take yourself back and imagine that you are at home playing in that warm, safe, relaxed environment, where the cat or dog is in the same room and it's all familiar, fun and relaxed. Remember – our brain doesn't know the difference between real and imaginary so paint a better picture for yourself.

4. **A good place.** What I mean by this is, create an image in your head where you perform well. It is all going perfectly, you are feeling good, relaxed and in control. There is nothing to worry about. Be happy, see it, believe it, picture it.

5. **It doesn't matter!** Exams and performances are important and we want to do our best, but in the grand scheme of things, we need to put this level of importance into perspective. Our lives don't depend on performing well. If you play or sing a wrong note the ground won't swallow you up, although you might like it to. My Dad always says, *'no one has been hurt'* or *'you haven't lost a limb'*. We need to keep things in perspective.

6. **Audience.** Sometimes you might think of your audience as judging you, and this is dangerous. None of us likes to be judged, An examiner isn't

CHOKING 65

judging you; he or she is simply marking your ability in that skill, against a set of criteria. An audience has come along to watch and enjoy your performance. They are wishing you well. An examiner and an audience are no different from you or me. They don't have special superhuman powers. They aren't going to set fire to you with their eyes or banish you to the outer solar system. They go to the toilet just like you and me! Think about that next time you have to perform – it will put a smile on your face and if we are smiling we aren't worrying. In fact they are usually worrying and thinking about themselves and not thinking about you at all.

7. **Centre.** When we are choking it is a high feeling, which is to say we feel it in our head. If we aren't feeling in control, we are probably thinking high – from our head, and even have a 'high' feeling. What we need to do is recognise this feeling and bring it downwards again to our centre, so we can regain control of ourselves. To do this, focus on your stomach or belly button, or even better your feet, so you can regain control. Try it now. Put your focus as high in your head as you can, keep your focus there and note how that feels. Then bring your focus down to your belly button; how does that feel different? Then finally put the focus in the arches of your feet. How much more in control do you feel than when you were thinking from high up in your head?

8. **Gratitude.** Feeling grateful for the things we have in our lives can help combat nerves and choking. Start with yourself and be grateful for you, your fingers so you can play, your voice so you can sing and speak, your legs so you can move, your eyes so you can see, your ears so you can hear. Then move on to your family, your friends, your peers, your pets and be thankful for what they do for you and how great they make you feel. Finally you might want to be thankful to the composers of the music that allows you to play and sing wonderful music or your favourite band, who create the music you love to listen to and sing along to. Being grateful and thankful stops us thinking about ourselves and combats nerves.

9. **A journey.** We use a lot of effort and time working towards a performance or exam and we can add unnecessary pressure by perceiving that goal as final, the end. All that work culminating in one moment. What a pressure. No wonder we choke. Instead, we need to look at the process

as a journey and the performance as a step along the way. That way it is just another lesson. Also, if you have worked so hard for one goal, when it is over there is a real disappointment or what we call an anticlimax. I have experienced this after performing in a show. You work so hard for one end goal that when it is over there is a real comedown. To help counteract this anticlimax and also choking we need to make sure that another goal or challenge is already in place before we complete this goal. A succession of goals would be even better, a bit like stepping stones across a river. That way this goal doesn't feel so final and we can continue on our journey.

10. **Breath.** When we are choking, our breath tends to be very shallow and short, when what will actually help us is long, deep, slow breathing. Why do deep breaths help ? Well, here is one answer.

    The vagus nerve – not vegas, as in Las Vegas, as I first thought when I heard it mentioned in a talk by John Rubin, on a 'Voice and The Brain' day run by AOTOS (Association of Teachers of Singing) in a very sunny and beautiful York. The vagus nerve interacts with all the organs of the body that it touches. It runs from our brain to our intestines and carries healing acetylcholine, which stops inflammation in the body caused by stress or worry and makes you feel relaxed. Acetylcholine is also responsible for learning and memory. We can't learn or heal if we are stressed. An easy way to activate the vagus nerve is to take a deep breath. A deep breath results in your cortisol levels reducing, your stress reducing and therefore you can heal. Meditation, relaxation and hypnotherapy can also help. Deep breathing has really helped my performances over the years, if I have ever been anxious.

18

Potential

We cannot allow one test or exam to measure our intelligence or ability now and for ever. No test or exam should ever be given that power to define you and your future. We can all grow, develop, learn and progress – we don't stand still. Just like everything in nature, we grow, and if we aren't growing, learning and improving we are getting worse, standing still or declining.

A test or exam shows you where you are at a specific point in time. It is a goal to aim for on our journey of perpetual learning. It doesn't show us what we are capable of in the future or even tomorrow. You will learn from today, which will make you a different person tomorrow. It can be used as feedback to show you where you must improve and learn, but also continue developing to greater achievement. A test shows us what we know and what we don't know at that point in time, and where we can improve.

> 'Potential is someone's capacity to develop their skills with effort over time.'
>
> CAROL DWECK, *MINDSET*

> 'You have to work hardest for the things you love most. And when it's music you love, you're in for the fight of your life.'
>
> NADJA SALERNO-SONNENBERG, VIOLINIST, NEW CENTURY CHAMBER ORCHESTRA

Believing that skills can be grown and developed helps people fulfil their potential. In *Drawing on the Right Side of the Brain*, Betty Edwards shows and teaches people the skills they need to draw in five days. This demonstrates how anyone can learn to draw by learning or knowing the skills and what to look for. This reinforces that we can learn anything if we want to, even if we begin with little or even no skill.

When people begin to play a musical instrument they don't know how to and have no skill to begin with. They have to learn that skill, the techniques, etc., just like learning to ride a bike, or even walking. There is no difference in learning to play an instrument or learning anything new. So surely this goes some way to prove that we are not born with a talent to play music, or run. Why would we be born with those skills, as opposed to being a 'natural walker'? You would never call anyone a natural walker, would you? No, because we all do it.

Adam Guettel is the grandson of Richard Rodgers, part of the musical composing duo Rodgers and Hammerstein who brought us musicals such as, 'The Sound of Music' and 'Oklahoma'. The pressure on him to be musical was quite significant, not least from his mother, Mary Rodgers, the daughter of Richard Rodgers, who said about her son, Adam, 'The talent is there and it's major'. His gift or 'talent' as his mother put it filled him with fear and he began running away from it. When Adam was 13 he was due to star in a TV movie but he cancelled saying that his voice had broken and he therefore couldn't sing the part. However, some years later he admitted that he had faked that his voice was changing because he couldn't handle the pressure. 'I wish I could just have fun and relax, and not have the responsibility of that potential to be some kind of great man'. The burden of 'talent' was killing his enjoyment. Several years later in 2005 he received two Tony Awards for his musical 'The Light in the Piazza', saying he realised that *'writing for character and telling stories through music was something that I really loved to do'*.

Carol Dweck, author of *Mindset: How You Can Fulfil Your Potential*, believes that there are two types of mindset, fixed and growth, and that depending on which you are will determine whether you reach your full potential or not. In her book she describes the two mindsets like this:

> **A fixed mindset** leads to a desire to look smarter, so challenges are avoided and they get defensive or give up easily when faced with obstacles. Effort is seen as fruitless and criticism is ignored and seen as useless. People feel threatened by others' success and the result is that they plateau early, not achieving their full potential.
>
> **A growth mindset** leads to a desire to learn and so embraces challenges and persists in the face of obstacles. Effort is seen as a path to mastery and criticism is used to learn from. People find lessons in others' success and the result is that they reach higher levels of achievement and potential.

Everyone begins their life with the potential of being musical, or anything else really. Along the way there are many factors that will influence that potential and determine the outcome.

Expert Musician

Our initial potential could result in creating an expert musician, which is in itself a culmination of many things. It's not only about playing or singing the right notes, listening, feeling and telling the story. Music has to 'paint a picture' for the listener and the player.

It's great to be a technical wizard, playing every note correctly and with precise rhythms, but this can sound mechanical, and in my opinion doesn't produce an expert musician. There needs to be feeling, passion and enjoyment to convey any meaning from music.

How do we 'paint a picture' with music? There is always a story to tell, a passion to convey, an emotion to explore.

We need to study the music and ask ourselves some questions:

- What is it about?
- What is the story the composer is telling?

Look at the:

- dynamics
- lyrics
- key signature
- time signature
- articulation
- title.

Find out about the:

- composer
- genre
- era.

If you create a picture in your own head of what the music means to you, there is more of a chance that the audience will connect with the music and you and understand the picture you are painting.

What makes an expert musician? Many things – here are some of my suggestions.

> playing
> listening feeling
> technique emotions creativity stick-to-it-ness
> caring memory
> theory passion
> patience belief
> motivation practice
> persistence

Passion

Is 'passion' the drive to persist? And, if so, where does it come from? Ellen Winner, a professor of psychology at Boston College, coined the phrase 'the rage to master'. She used this to describe the passion and drive felt, that is seen by some children to work in a particular field from a very young age. Some children need no encouragement to practise and if we really think about what the children are doing it's not even seen or perceived as practice is it? It is just a child's desire to do something of their own accord using their initiative. They enjoy it and because they are doing this thing for many hours from a very young age they then in turn accomplish greatness and success ahead of others of the same age.

As I've said before my parents aren't sporty therefore I never really watched, participated in or took an interest in sport, except dance – although that is more of an art than a sport. This was reflected at school as I wasn't any good at sport. I would be the last one in the cross country, even having taken the short cut, with my best friend coming first. I had no real interest in sports and used the excuse I wasn't any good and that was that. I did try, but I never put in any significant 'practice' so therefore didn't improve.

> **'A father cannot criticise a son for not playing football if he doesn't play football with him and encourage him.'**
>
> **LISA FAYE BROADHEAD**

My interests lay in music, acting and dancing, initially spurred on by my parents' encouragement and then later on by teachers at my infant and junior school who saw my enthusiasm for the arts and did all they could to support and nurture that interest. I remember being the Sun, Frosty The Snowman and then Benjamin in 'Joseph and the Amazing Technicolor Dreamcoat' in school productions.

Passion develops. It doesn't wake up one day and say here I am! Encouragement in childhood is imperative, but don't push too hard or the child may kick back and resent you. Remember – people work passionately on their own ideas, projects and goals, not those thrust upon them by others. We all want to do things we enjoy and believe in and feel there is a reason for doing.

I can't sing songs that I can't connect with or believe in. I remember being given a new song to learn at The Royal Academy of Music where I was studying for a Postgraduate Diploma specialising in Musical Theatre. I didn't like the song, although it was musical theatre, it was an older song and I didn't feel I could connect with the style so found singing it very difficult. I just didn't believe in it. This goes back to Kenneth Robinson and his belief that finding our 'element' is the key to our success and happiness. The song given to me didn't fit with my love for musical theatre. Of course we need to try new things, or we could be missing out on finding our 'element' altogether, but this could go some way to explain why we have a passion for some things and not others. I prefer to sing songs that are positive or make me and my audience think about our lives. However, the songs I sing quite often change with my mood, hence sometimes I can't decide what songs to sing until the day of the gig, which is fine when I work alone, but not so easy when you work with others.

Quite often the hobbies and interests we have as a child, sometimes even before school starts, focus the direction we take in adult life and if they don't become our careers they become our hobbies, quite often on a serious level.

> **am·a·teur** *noun* /a-mə-[ˌ]tər/ a person who does something (such as a sport or hobby) for pleasure and not as a job

Amateur derives from the Latin word amator, which means lover, devoted friend, or someone in pursuit of an objective. An amateur is someone who does an activity for the love of it. This doesn't mean they put in any less effort or aren't as good, but that they just choose to follow this pursuit in their spare time and make their money from another job. Perhaps this 'thing' is their 'element'– it doesn't have to be their job.

Pro-ams are those who pursue an activity like an amateur, but to a professional level, and mainly for the love of it rather than the monetary reward. They will usually only make a small income from their pastime, although the level of commitment and time is at a professional level, as is generally the outcome too.

Professionals are those who engage in an activity for gain or as a means of livelihood, that is, they are paid for their work. A professional is someone who is a member of a profession.

Passion killers

Why do some people put others down? In order to make themselves feel better?

People put others down and stamp on their passion because they either don't understand or don't want you to become better than them. If you start improving or learning new exciting skills, you might leave them behind – and where does that leave them? Instead of putting others down, raise your own standards to their level or beyond. This way you will be growing and learning.

Negativity achieves nothing. We sometimes need to cry or have a moan, but then we have to move on. Pick yourself up, dust yourself off, and start all over again, as the song says. Continuing on a negative path is a downward spiral that will only make you feel worse. It doesn't make you feel better when you go on and on about something or go over it again and again in your head. You have to break the record, so to speak, as we discovered earlier, in creating a new habit. Smile, do something wacky, strange, go outside and take a walk. There is a way out but the only person who can change your feelings in the end is you. Complaining about things doesn't make it better in the long run, except momentarily, but to keep going over and over things is only bad news. You need to look for a solution, or at least make a change. It's a little like if you don't like a TV show. Turn it off or tune into a new channel. There are plenty of other programmes so you don't have to watch it. Somebody else does like it otherwise it wouldn't exist.

There are fabulous people out there who are doing and achieving great things, making this world better – but also sadly these people are often ridiculed by those who don't appreciate or understand their efforts. And once again it is harder work to raise their own standards than mock those of others – the easy way out.

We have the power to change our outlook and feelings in a second so we shouldn't blame our circumstances or someone or something else, as it's up to us to change things. Quite often our circumstance is due to a decision we made or didn't make further down the line. And if your circumstance isn't your fault, does sitting around and blaming everyone else help you? No, you have to find the courage to pick yourself up and change your situation.

We have to take responsibility for our actions ourselves. If we are fat it's because we eat the wrong food, or too much food and don't exercise enough, not that we have big bones, which is what I believed for a long while. Yes, you will have a body shape similar to that of your parents, but that shouldn't be used as an excuse. It's more that we are adopting the habits of those around us as we are influenced by our environment. We use the excuse that we smoke, eat too much, take drugs because of something that happened in our past. Perhaps this is true, but you have chosen to make that your excuse because it lets you off the hook. It makes us feel like it isn't our fault, which in turn means that we don't have to do anything about it or change it because we can't. This is the same with our excuses as to why we aren't the musicians we want to be or why we don't put in the required practice.

Allowing the past to rule the future or even today is not something that we have to accept. A boat is not powered by its wake, it is powered by energy – fuel – that's what propels the boat forward, not the wake, the past! It's what's happening now that's important and where you have chartered the course of your boat, your life. How many times have I read or heard the words '*If you fail to plan, you plan to fail*', but how true they are. So don't allow something in your past to hold you back today and into your future. The past is exactly that – past. Now move on!

Butterflies and Voices

We have all felt nervous at one time or another but what exactly is it that makes us have that funny feeling in our stomach?

When we are nervous, there is a tickling, fluttering feeling in our stomach, hence we say we've got butterflies. What is actually happening is our sympathetic nervous system has kicked in to increase our levels of alertness to help us perform at our best in a certain situation. So when we are doing something that is important to us and we want to do our best, blood is being sent to our brain and to our muscles to prepare us for action. As a result, a lot of blood is squeezed out of the vessels that wrap around our intestines, producing the fluttering feeling in our stomachs.

In fact what we sometimes perceive as a bad feeling, when we experience butterflies, is actually a very positive sign, as our bodies are getting us ready for the activity.

Nerves can also be brought about by that little voice inside our head. You know the one – it tells you to do something, or not do something and you procrastinate. I know from my own experience how that little voice can affect my performance.

This happened to me at a function where I was singing back in 2013. It was actually a very relaxed outdoor charity function for a friend who works in broadcasting, and all was going very well. However, part way through my second set I was convinced that the singer Lulu had just entered the area where I was singing. What happened? I panicked and thought crikey I have to impress, sound great. My mind was interfering with me. Instead of thinking about singing the song I was at that moment in mid flow of performing, my mind was chatting to me about what song I should sing next. 'Don't for goodness' sake sing "Shout"' – Lulu's hit from the 60s, the voice in my head said to me! As a result, everything tightened, not only my mind but my throat and when I went for the high note in the song, it just wasn't quite there, because I wasn't focusing on it. It was bad, or at least it was in my head. I sang the next song walking through the audience to check out if it really was Lulu, and it wasn't. I breathed a sigh of relief. Now normal service could be resumed, I stopped choking, stopped listening to that annoying voice in my head and finished the evening to rapturous applause, huge congratulations and helped to raise an awful lot of money for a well deserving charity.

I have learned the hard way that my mind and that little voice are powerful things and can make me act in a particular way. If I talk to myself in a certain way about a specific subject, then I know now that it affects me. Up until that point I hadn't realised how powerful that little voice could be. The voice in my head was giving me feedback, whether I wanted it or not, and it was internal, biased and not honest at all.

Practice Tips

I am pretty sure that at no point did anyone say that practice must be dull, boring, painful and mind numbing. It should be exciting, challenging and fun. You don't have to be serious and tense in order to learn and in fact the exact opposite is required as we have discovered. If we are tense, the chances are we really aren't learning anything.

1. Playing games
Practising our pieces or scales, for example, should mean playing with them, so we get to know them better. We could do a quick quiz on the piece and ask questions like why did the composer put that note there? Can I play it louder, quieter, quicker, slower? What happens when we play the piece faster or slower?

Try these ideas out next time you practise:

A. Play with only three fingers on each hand.
B. Record yourself, then play a duet with yourself.
C. Sing and play at the same time (obviously difficult if you are playing a wind instrument!).
D. Work out the chords and just play them.
E. Cross your hands over.
F. Video yourself and watch back, giving yourself feedback.
G. Sing or play along with your favourite artist.
H. Sing/play as fast as you can – and then as slow as you can.
I. Make up lyrics to your piece of music.

Playing a musical instrument or singing is like playing a board game or a video game.

A. The more we play the game, the better we become (that's called practice, although I've never heard any of my students say 'I'm practising Minecraft', they say, 'I'm playing Minecraft').

B. There are other players or opponents whom we try to be better than in order to win the game, as it were. So we should check out the competition, where they are in the game and look at how they got there. Studying our opponents can make it quicker for us to get to the top so we can win the game.

Before learning a new piece or song we should look at the structure, then we will be more prepared for what is coming up in the piece and it won't be such a surprise! Look out for:

A. Repetitions of notes and short phrases.
B. Sections of scales or arpeggios.
C. How the music moves – whether in steps or jumps.

2. Goals and football

When a goal is scored in football it is because a team has worked together to achieve that result. As with football, working on musical goals as a group, team or in pairs, can have a similar result. By working together towards one goal, you can gauge how you are doing alongside others, which will also push you. The goal could have a reward linked to it once reached. In football it is winning a championship and a cup. For you it could be winning your favourite chocolate bar, but even the satisfaction of reaching the goal in itself can be reward enough. Make sure though that you create achievable goals. They shouldn't be so hard that you give up trying, but also not so easy that you aren't challenged and don't learn anything.

   Picture a path to your goal. Why are you practising? Because your teacher has told you to? No, it needs to be because you tell yourself 'practice will make me improve, I will be able to play that particular piece well, I will get a higher exam result, I have a concert, performance, I want to ...'. It's up to you. Musicians like Jools Holland will practise for up to eight hours every day, just like professional footballers.

   A football player's goal might be the match on Saturday, or the World Cup qualifiers. That goal is not moveable, so the player has to keep up with the practice to ensure he is ready to play at his very best when the time comes for it. That is why goals, like exams and performances, are good targets. They are immoveable and focus our attention.

Goals are only achieved through definite plans, backed by desire and constant earnest practice! A footballer can't go out and kick a ball a few times and expect to be able to score goals.

3. A plan

> 'A goal without a plan is just a wish.'
>
> **ANTOINE DE SAINT-EXUPÉRY, FRENCH NOVELIST**

In order to achieve our goals we need a plan. Footballers have a strategy plan, put in place by their manager, as to who will play in what position, etc. in order to score goals. If we don't have a plan, we don't know how to reach our goal. Think of it like a map that we use to get us from A to B. This is exactly the same. Create a plan to practise at regular intervals. Set out specific times each day and what you want to achieve in that time.

4. Keep on track

By setting out a plan you can keep on track. Sometimes you might take a slightly different route but by keeping a practice diary you can ensure that you are achieving the results required to reach your goal on time and fully equipped to face the music!

- A. **Measure practice.** Keep a record of your practice – time of day, which days, how long?
- B. **Measure success.** Keep a record of your progress – what you achieve, use tick boxes.
- C. **Measure performance.** Keep a record of performances – how did it go, feedback?

5. Listening

Listening to recordings of the music you are playing or singing is vital. It helps build up a mental map of where we are aiming for and etches the piece of music on our brain. Today, music is more accessible than ever before. YouTube, Spotify and iTunes all mean that we can download music

6. Mentally practise

in seconds and listen to it wherever we are. There really isn't any excuse for not listening to what we are working on and we should be listening to this every day.

6. Mentally practise

Sports people use mental practice to help learn their skills, by rehearsing the physical action in their mind. We can play back our scales, pieces and songs in our mind, focusing on which finger goes on which note, or where a song goes up and down. Mentally singing the song or piece of music, or even picturing the music and its lyrics in your mind's eye really helps to concrete it in. Try it!

> **Exercise**
> Place your hands on your instrument and close your eyes. Without looking for the notes, or at your hands, I want you to feel your way around. Practise jumping from one note to the next note and then up the degrees of the scale, so eventually you are jumping a whole octave. You must not move onto the next degree of the scale until you have jumped the previous distance correctly five times. If you make an error you have to start again at one.
>
> This exercise helps you move around your instrument more freely. Not having to look at your hands when playing gives you freedom, as you feel and sense where you need to move to.

7. Mime

> **mime** *verb* /mʌɪm/
> 1. use only gesture and movement to act out (a play or role)
> 2. pretend to sing or play an instrument as a recording is being played

For example, right now mime drinking a cup of tea. You can quite easily picture it in your mind's eye and then carry out the movements required to pick up the imaginary tea cup, bring it to your mouth without spilling a drop and then take a drink – careful, it might be hot! You can quite easily mime drinking a cup of tea because you have done it so many times before and it has become natural or instinctive.

> **Exercise**
> Mime playing or singing a C major scale. Notice how your fingers, throat, mouth and body move. This is a great exercise to see if you really do know your scales. If you can't mime them, then you don't know them.

8. Memorise

I know the British National Anthem off by heart. I didn't learn it by sitting down and memorising it on purpose. I learned it at school through weekly repetition and I can now recite it without having to consciously think about what line is coming next. It just flows. That is how singing the lyrics of a song should be – they should just flow. Only then when you aren't having to consciously think of what is coming next, can you actually think about the text and put it into context.

> Memorise the text
> So you don't have to think what's next
> And you can concentrate on the context

For singing, acting and dancing this is imperative. If you are thinking about notes, counting and technique, you can't concentrate on telling the story. What slows fingers down is not knowing where to put them. We have to put in the practice before the performance.

9. Subconscious

Practising also means that certain skills can move into our subconscious. This is where our mind gets to work, in the background, doing things we don't really need to put our full focus on, like using a fork for example. You don't have to think about using a fork because you practised, or tried, tried and tried again to use it correctly and you mastered using that fork so now you can use it without consciously thinking about it. It's the same as riding a bike or driving a car. Once you have mastered it, your subconscious just gets on with it, so you can focus on other things. That is how singing and playing should feel – effortless mastery – so you don't have to consciously think about it, you just do it.

> **Exercise**
> Sometimes we try too hard and this can hamper our progress. Try looking out of the back of your head, or imagining that there is a window back there, that is open and then play or sing a section. How free does that feel? Slightly lighter in the head and easier? That is because you have put your consciousness further away and that annoying little voice can't interfere with what you are trying so hard to achieve.

10. Myelin

Remember that what you practise will stay encoded in your memory. As we get better and better, consolidating what we have learned before, the myelin in our brains gets bigger, a little bit like building a brick wall. You start with one line of bricks and build on it. If you don't practise it's like taking that first row of bricks away and starting again. You will never build a wall – or myelin – this way. Even builders practise how to make the best cement to make the bricks stick and the best technique to make the wall straight. We all practise skills every day to improve but most of the time we don't think of what we are doing as practice. We build skills, techniques and generally improve in everyday things like cooking, baking, putting on make up, driving a car, riding a bike, working an iPad, playing Minecraft. Absolutely everything we do involves practice, but most of the time we just don't realise it.

11. Practise on the days you eat

It's no good suddenly practising the day before your music lesson! Any music teacher can tell and the only person you are letting down is yourself. Little and often is better than all at once at the last minute! It's the only way to build myelin. As Shinichi Suzuki says, *'Practise on the days you eat'*.

12. Counting

Count repetitions, not minutes, or time. If you sit there for 20 minutes and only play something once, is that 20 minutes of practice? It's far better to count how many times you play something. It isn't the practice that's important, it's what you do in that practice.

13. Copying
Copy out your piece of music or song. By copying out the piece that you are working on, you are having to really read the notes and lyrics. This will help you to recognise any similarities or patterns and build up a mental picture of the piece.

14. Make a jigsaw
Once you've copied out the piece, cut it up into sections, like a jigsaw. Then just practise a piece of the jigsaw at a time. This will stop you from moving ahead before you have really worked on that section, and you can also create a whole new piece or song. It really is a lot of fun!

15. Semitone steps
In the same way that a semitone is the smallest step that you can make on a piano, take only semitone steps in your practice. Perfect one small step at a time. Get it 100% correct and then move on.

16. The tortoise and the hare
In the Aesop Fable of the tortoise and the hare, the fast hare brags about his speed and challenges anyone to race with him. The tortoise takes up the challenge and the race begins. Having raced ahead, the confident hare lies down to have a nap, only to wake to find that the constant tortoise has overtaken him. Now the hare cannot catch the tortoise up to win the race, and the slow, steady tortoise is victorious. The moral of the story? Constant wins the race! Take your time, rather than racing ahead, and don't be lazy.

17. How slowly?
'Slowly' really is a fantastic tool to have in our musical practice bag. When we play slowly it highlights every note, stimulating us to focus. Our attention to detail is heightened and if we can play it slowly perfectly then we can definitely play it at breakneck speed perfectly.

18. Use similes
If you are struggling to play something slower, picture a tortoise slowly going on its way, and play like a tortoise. If you need to speed up and be

lighter with your touch or words you could play and sing like the hare or Singing Sam.

Here are some other ideas:

Staccato. Imagine that whatever you touch is hot, or the tip of your tongue is hot.
Legato. This is smooth and connected like a winding stream or river. Calm and flowing.
Slur. Think of a slug (this one I have taken from one of my young creative students). A slug is slimy and slides along the ground, leaving its silvery trail, joining everything together.

Try making up your own similes and see how creating a picture in your mind helps. You could even draw a picture at the side of your music (in pencil) as a reminder.

19. Don't ignore a mistake
If you accidentally spill something on the floor, like a drink, you wouldn't ignore it would you? No, you would clean it up. Or if you broke a friend's favourite ornament you would try and fix it. The same applies to music. If you make a mistake then stop and sort it out there and then. It will only get worse if you leave it – just like the spilt drink or the broken ornament. What happens if your friend finds out? Better to be honest and deal with it, rather than pretend it didn't happen.

20. Power of seven
Repetition shouldn't be seen as a chore but as a very powerful tool in your practice bag. Once you have sorted out a mistake and performed the section perfectly, do it again a further seven times perfectly. This is the magic power of seven. Doing it correctly once won't mean that it won't go wrong again, whereas doing it a further seven times correctly will mean Max Myelin can come into play.

21. End on a high note
This should be taken quite literally. Make sure that the last thing you do in a practice session is to finish on something that you do well, enjoy and can have fun with!

Conclusion

No doubt by now you will have come to your own conclusion as to whether music is a 'talent' or a result of practice.

For me from my research over the past two years and teaching over the past 18 years, I have come to the conclusion that the word talent has been misused. As we have discovered, our upbringing and our environment, not our genes, determine how we end up. Talent is actually the ability to put one's mind to practice and has nothing to do with being born with a gift. We should be replacing the word 'talent' with 'effort', because that is what talent is – effort. However, *Britain's Got Effort* doesn't have quite the same ring to it, although it would certainly send out a better message.

TALENT = PRACTICE   or   PRACTICE = TALENT

Talent is a result of commiting to practice excellence, to working hard to pursue and achieve your goals, by setting out a plan.

> **'We are what we repeatedly do. Excellence, then, is not an act but a habit.'**
>
> **ARISTOTLE**

Neurological research now shows that every normal, healthy human being is musical (Welch, 2001; Zatorre and Peretz, 2001). It is part of our human design. Music is there for everyone to make, create and enjoy and not just for the select few. We are all musical and we just need the opportunity for our musicality to be celebrated and developed (Welch, 2001).

CONCLUSION

It seems to me that practice is perceived as a bad word and talent as a good word. Is that because the word practice isn't very dynamic and exciting, and means hard work whereas talent conjures up pleasing images of fame and ease? Also, most of us have been led to believe that if we have to practise something then we aren't talented, but as we now know we aren't talented unless we practise. What we need to do is change our perceptions. Practice is a great creative process involving learning, discovering, problem solving, perfecting, enjoying and experimenting. In fact it's actually the story you tell yourself about why you need to practise or do anything that will get you to do it successfully and enjoy the process. Change the story and you change the outcome. Change the word and we change the attitude. From now on I'm choosing a more dynamic word.

PRACTICE =

achieve
work out create
persist go for broke
conquer win master develop outshine
take part get in there
go for it

The 5678 Music Tree

Why is my logo a music tree?
Like a tree, we grow. A tree grows bigger and stronger and sends out more branches as it grows. How does it grow? It starts off life as a tiny seed, and with the right amount of water, nutrients in the soil, air, sun and environment it grows little by little, branch by branch. Also, what we don't see are the roots, getting stronger and longer and bigger under the ground. What is happening underneath is making the tree above the ground bigger and stronger. The tree changes and develops constantly, sometimes bearing fruit and flowers, other times shedding its leaves.
This is the same for our musical ability, or any ability. It starts off with a little bit of interest just like a small seed. Then this is fed by exposure to music, listening, teaching, nurturing and placing in the correct environment. The more we feed that initial interest, the more it grows bigger and stronger. And just like the roots of a tree, our practice is making sure our technique is solid and deep by creating a strong foundation on top of which our musical ability is flourishing and ever changing. As the seasons make the leaves change colour, fall and grow again, so does our own musical ability grow, sometimes scaling back and then with renewed energy we grow once again.

Bibliography

Bateson, Patrick. 2000. *Design For A Life: How Behaviour and Personality Develop*. Simon & Schuster.

Bengtsson, S. L., Nagy, Z., Skare, S., Forsman, L., Forssberg, H. & Ullén, F. 2005. 'Extensive piano practicing has regionally specific effects on white matter development.' *Nature Neuroscience*, 8, 1148–50.

Binet, A. 1909, reprinted 1973. *Les idées modernes sur les enfants (Modern Ideas on Children)*. Flammarion.

Binet, A. (trans. Simmel, M. L. & Barron, S.). 1966. *Mnemonic Virtuosity: A Study of Chess Players*. Journal Press.

Coyle, D. 2012. *The Little Book of Talent: 52 Tips For Improving Skills*. Random House.

Coyle, D. 2009. *The Talent Code: Greatness Isn't Born. It's Grown. Here's How*. Bantam.

Craft, A., Jeffrey, R. & Leibling, M. 2001. *Creativity in Education*. Continuum.

Davidson, R. J., Jackson, D. C. & Kalin, E. H. 2000. 'Emotion, plasticity, context and regulation: Perspectives from affective neuroscience.' *Psychological Bulletin* 126, 6, 890–909.

Design For A Life. A Talk With Patrick Bateson. The Edge.

Dweck, C. 2012. *Mindset: How You Can Fulfil Your Potential*. Random House Publishing.

Ericsson, K. A., Krampe, R. Th. & Tesch-Römer, C. 1993. 'The Role of Deliberate Practice in the Acquisition of Expert Performance.' *Psychological Review* 100, 3, 363–406.

Gladwell, M. 2009. *Outliers: The Story of Success*. Penguin.

Henriksson-Macaulay, L. 2014. *The Music Miracle: The Scientific Secret to Unlocking Your Child's Full Potential*. Earnest House Publishing.

Hill, N. 2007. *Think And Grow Rich*. Wilder Publications.

Homer. 2003. *The Odyssey* (ed. P. Jones, trans. E. V. Rieu). Penguin Classics.

Houseman, B. 2002. *Finding Your Voice: A Complete Voice Training Manual for Actors*. Nick Hern Books.

Lemov, D. 2010. *Teach Like a Champion: 49 Techniques that Put Students on the Path to College*. Jossey-Bass.

Lemov, D., Woolway, E. & Yezzi, K. 2012. *Practice Perfect: 42 Rules for Getting Better at Getting Better*. Jossey-Bass.

Levitin, D. J. 2008. *This is Your Brain on Music: Understanding a Human Obsession*. Atlantic Books.

Lichtman, J. 2009. 'Neuroscience: Making Connections.' *Nature News*. Quoted in Robinson, K. *Out of Our Minds: Learning to Be Creative*. Capstone.
NACCCE. 1999. 'All Our Futures: Creativity, Culture and Education.' DFEE.
Robinson, K. 2001. *Out of Our Minds: Learning to Be Creative*. Capstone.
Rodgers, R. & Hammerstein, O. 1949. 'You've Got to Be Carefully Taught' from *South Pacific*. Williamson Music.
Schlaug, G., Norton, A., Overy, K. & Winner, E. 2005. 'Effects of music training on the child's brain and cognitive development.' *Annals of the New York Academy of Sciences*, 1060, 219–30.
Shenk, D. 2010. *The Genius in All of Us: Why Everything You've Been Told About Genes, Talent and Intelligence is Wrong*. Icon Books.
Sondheim, S. 1986. 'Children Will Listen' from *Into the Woods*. Rilting Music Inc. Warner Bros Publications.
Suzuki, S. 1990. *Man and Talent: Search for the Unknown*. Shar Publications.
Suzuki, S. 1986 (2nd ed.). *Nurtured by Love: The Classic Approach to Talent Education*. Suzuki Method International.
Welch, G. 2005. *The Misunderstanding of Music*. Institute of Education. University of London.

Other sources & further reading
Am I Tone Deaf? – BBC 4 Radio Programme. First broadcast 9 September 2011.
Ball, P. 2011. *The Music Instinct: How Music Works and Why We Can't Do Without It*. Vintage Books.
Bloom, B. 1985. *Developing Talent in Young People*. Ballantine Books.
Byrne, D. 2012. *How Music Works*. Canongate Books Ltd.
Colvin, G. 2008. *Talent Is Overrated: What Really Separates World-Class Performers from Everybody Else*. Nicholas Brealey Publishing Ltd.
Csikszentmihalyi, M., Rathunde, K. & Whalen, S. 1996. *Talented Teenagers: The Roots of Success and Failure*. Cambridge University Press.
Gallwey, W. T. & Green, B. 2003. *The Inner Game of Music*. Pan.
Galton, F. *Hereditary Genius: An Inquiry into its Laws and Consequences*. First published in 1869. www.mugu.com/galton/books/hereditary-genius/galton-1869-Hereditary_Genius.pdf (Accessed 13 November 2014).
Gardner, H. *The MI Theory*. www.multipleintelligencetheory.co.uk (Accessed 13 November 2014).

Gerver, R. 2010. *Creating Tomorrow's Schools Today: Education, Our Children, Their Futures*. Continuum.
Klickstein, G. 2009. *The Musician's Way: A Guide to Practice, Performance, and Wellness*. Oxford University Press.
Lewis, J. & Webster, A. 2014. *Sort Your Brain Out: Boost Your Performance, Manage Stress and Achieve More*. Capstone.
Peters, S. 2012. *The Chimp Paradox: The Mind Management Programme to Help You Achieve Success, Confidence and Happiness*. Vermilion.
Robbins, A. New edition 2001. *Awaken the Giant Within*. Pocket Books.
Robbins, A. 2001. *Unlimited Power: The New Science of Personal Achievement*. Pocket Books.
Robinson, K. 2009. *The Element: How Finding Your Passion Changes Everything*. Penguin Books.
Sacks, O. 2011. *Musicophilia: Tales of Music and the Brain*. Picador.
Stigler, J. W. & Hiebert, J. 1999. *The Teaching Gap: Best Ideas from the World's Teachers for Improving Education in the Classroom*. The Free Press.
Syed, M. 2011. *Bounce: The Myth of Talent and the Power of Practice*. Fourth Estate.
Weisberg, R. W. 2006. *Creativity: Understanding Innovation in Problem Solving, Science, Invention, and the Arts*. John Wiley & Sons.
Werner, K. 1990. *Effortless Mastery: Liberating the Master Musician Within*. Jamey Aebersold Jazz.

Index

amateurs 73
Aristotle 86
autopilot 24–5, 37

Bateson, Patrick 14
Beatles, The 45
Beethoven, Ludwig Van 61
belief 42–4, 67
Bernstein, Leonard 30–1
brain 17, 18, 19, 38
Broadhead, Lisa Faye 72
Button, Jenson 38

childhood, child prodigies 17–18, 32–6
choking 62–6
chunking 49–50
Coyle, Daniel 40

dancing 17
Disney, Walt 61
Dweck, Carol 59, 67, 68–9

Earnest Practice 37, 40, 46, 48
Edison, Thomas 55
Edwards, Betty 68
80–20 rule 50
element, being in our 30, 73, 74
environment 13, 14, 15, 16–18, 29, 32–6, 47, 75
Ericsson, K. Anders 33, 37, 46
experience 29–31

feedback 55–8, 59–61, 67
Ford, Henry 61

Galton, Francis 13, 27
Gardner, Howard 28
genes 13–15
Gladwell, Malcolm 45
goals 41–4, 79–80
God-given talent 11, 32
Guettel, Adam 68

Henriksson-Macaulay, Liisa 11
Homer 11
Houseman, Barbara 63

IQ (intelligence quotient) 26–8

Jesus 10

Lang Lang 47
Levitin, Daniel Joseph 36
Lewis, Clive Staples 43
Lichtman, Jeff W. 22
Lloyd Webber, Andrew 29
Lulu 76–7

MI Theory (Multiple Intelligence Theory) 28
mime 81
mindset 68–9
Mozart, Wolfgang Amadeus 32–3, 46
musical ear 51–4
myelin 20–22, 82

nature versus nurture 13–15, 27
nerves 25, 76–7

Overy, Katie 17

Pareto, Vilfredo 50
passion 72–5
potential 67–9, 70
practice 6, 7–8, 23–5, 33, 37–40, 45–8, 61, 78–85, 87
praise 59–60
Presley, Elvis 61

Robinson, Kenneth 30, 31, 73

Salerno-Sonnenberg, Nadja 67
school 34–6
Shenk, David 16
singing 9, 11, 16, 42–3, 51–4, 76–7

Socrates 36
Sondheim, Stephen 60
Streisand, Barbra 45
Suzuki, Shinichi 32, 46–7, 83

talent 6, 10–12, 13–15, 32, 33, 68, 86
10,000 hour rule, the 45
tone deafness 51–4
Tyler, S.W. 24

Ullén, Fredrik 21
University of London 12

Welch, Graham 12
Winner, Ellen 72

Acknowledgements

Text permissions

The author wishes to thank the following people who have given their permission for extracts to be used in this book:

p. 12 Professor Graham F. Welch; p. 14 Professor Patrick Bateson; p. 16 David Shenk; p. 22 Jeff W. Lichtman; pp. 30, 31 Sir Kenneth Robinson; pp. 33, 37 Dr K. Anders Ericsson; p. 36 Daniel J. Levitin; p. 40 Daniel Coyle – *The Talent Code*; pp. 46, 47 International Suzuki Association; pp. 59, 67 Carol Dweck; p. 61 NACCCE report – Sir Kenneth Robinson; p. 61 Bob Jeffrey, *Creativity in Education*; p. 63 Barbara Houseman, voice and acting coach, *Finding Your Voice*; p. 67 Nadja Salerno-Sonnenberg, violinist, New Century Chamber Orchestra.

Every effort has been made to obtain permission and apologies are offered to anyone whom it has not been possible to contact.